TRAMLINES TO T

George White of Bristol

GW00360987

GEORGE WHITE

redcliffe

First published in 1995
by Redcliffe Press Ltd.,
22 Canynge Square, Bristol

© Sir George White, Bart

ISBN 1 872971 73 3

British Library Cataloguing in Publication Data
A catalogue record for this book is available from
the British Library

All rights reserved. No part of this publication may be
reproduced, stored in a retrieval system, or transmitted in
any form or by any means, electronic, mechanical,
photocopying, recording or otherwise, without the prior
permission of the publishers.

Typeset by Mayhew Typesetting, Rhayader, Powys
Printed in Great Britain by The Longdunn Press, Bristol

GEORGE WHITE
1905

A portrait by the society photographers Lafayette of New Bond Street, London.

*To (George) Philip, Caroline, Katie, Daphne and Robert: his descendants,
And to Lisa, with love.*

The Heights by great men reached and kept
Were not sustained by sudden flight,
But they, while their companions slept
Were toiling upwards in the night.
[Henry Wadsworth Longfellow 1807−1882]

PREFACE

My grandfather died in 1964, when I was sixteen. He was a very private man of whom James Wentworth Day, aeronautical correspondent of the *Daily Mail* had once written "it would be easier for a newspaper man to go into the presence of the Grand Lama of Tibet than for a pencil to wag inquisitively beneath the discouraging eye of Sir G. Stanley White Bt." He had served as managing director of both the British and Colonial Aeroplane Company and the Bristol Aeroplane Company since 1911. With his uncle Samuel White and his cousin Sir William Verdon-Smith as successive chairmen, he had built up the enterprise at Filton to be one of the largest aeronautical sites in the world by the end of the Second World War. He had presided over the production of aircraft from the Bristol Boxkite (made from cotton, wood and piano wire and capable of 45 m.p.h.), to the Bristol 188 (made from puddle-welded stainless steel and capable of Mach 2).

It was clear from the way in which he lived and from the way others treated him that he was a remarkable man, though I never once heard him claim any credit for his achievements. It was his father, he said, who had been responsible for it all.

I longed to know more, to find out who his father was and what he did, but I was as reserved as my grandfather, and I did not like to ask questions. When I did, he would reply simply that it was all long past and that it "was better to let sleeping dogs lie". When I asked his formidable sister, with whom I got on very well, except when discussing this particular subject, she would reply that I was speaking of her father and not of mine: and there the matter would rest.

As the years passed, I found my widowed grandmother only too happy to answer any question I asked, because she was immensely proud of her father-in-law and had witnessed many of his later triumphs. But by then, as a typical late-teenager, I was less interested. I threw away the opportunities I had to listen to tales of the Army manoeuvres of September 1910, of the Circuit de l'Europe Air Race in 1911, of early pilots, of pioneer aircraft designers and of aeronautical adventures which she remembered so clearly. So it is that in later years I have had to find out for myself.

The brief account I offer here began as a lecture, written for the Bristol Aero Collection. It is intended to give a broad impression of George White's life and not in any way to supplant the definitive works on his business achievements by Dr. Charles Harvey and Dr. Jon Press in *Studies in the Business History of Bristol* (1988) or *Sir George White of Bristol* (1989). It is based where possible on primary sources, but also many secondary sources which I have gathered together and acknowledged in the footnotes. It is clear from the quantity of George White's papers which remain unread from the turn of the century, that my account only scratches the surface of his life. I hope however that it will help to inspire further research and to restore him to the position which he deserves in the history of his native city and of his country.

I am very grateful for all the help I have received, especially from the staff of the Bristol Record Office, where most of George White's papers reside. I am grateful too to the Trustees and Team of the Bristol Aero Collection and the members of the Rolls-Royce Heritage Trust, who encouraged me to begin. I am grateful to Peter Brown, whose thoughtful and continuing research on all the members of my family who have been involved in the aircraft industry encouraged me to make sense of the family papers which were in my care. I am grateful to Penelope Mellor, for her expert advice on Cotham. Finally I am grateful to Brown Shipley Stockbroking Ltd and Veale Wasbrough, solicitors as well as to British Aerospace, Filton, and to Rolls-Royce, Patchway (heirs of the Bristol Aeroplane Company), whose generosity has enabled this work to be published. Long may the aircraft industry at Filton prosper.

George White F.S.A. 1995.

"**B**ristol awoke on Thursday morning," wrote a *Bristol Guardian* correspondent on November 24th 1916, "to find itself in the shadow of a great loss. . . It was as though some familiar, pervading and indispensable activity amongst us had ceased without warning and without explanation. Then came realisation, and with it the sense of bereavement, of deprivation. We had lost the greatest man amongst us; Sir George White was dead."[1]

Obituaries in at least one hundred and eighteen British newspapers echoed similar sentiments. "He touched nothing he did not vivify," said one, "and his activities were so intimately in contact with Bristol life, that his death brought home a sense of personal and civic loss in a fashion without parallel in our day."[2]

A simple private funeral was held at St. Mary's, Stoke Bishop, at the wish of his family, but at the same time a "vast congregation" of Bristolians attended a memorial service at the Cathedral. "There was such a large gathering of representatives of civic and public life, religious institutions, hospitals and other forms of philanthropy, as well as educational, commercial and other interests, that for a memorial service to a private citizen the occasion was unique." Flags were flown at half-mast on public buildings and, throughout the city, trams decked in black crepe ribbons stopped in respectful silence. The passengers and staff alighted and stood bareheaded in the streets.[3]

Canon Everingham, with typical Edwardian Imperial pride, declared from his Bristol pulpit that "George White's influence, like that of Cabot and Colston, has been felt throughout the country as a man of foresight, enterprise, and bold venture; in fact as a leader of men. What Cecil Rhodes was to South Africa, what Herbert Kitchener was to Egypt, George White was in great measure to this nation and to Bristol in particular."[4] News of his death found space in newspapers from Quebec[5] to *The Times of India*.

George White's family was not from Bristol, but had originated in Devon. His grandfather, Henry White, had been born at Cullompton in 1787, and had moved to Honiton some time before 1811. There he had married Elizabeth Tucker. They lived at No. 10 New Street, a tiny house just off the busy London to Exeter coaching road, and derived their income from transport. Surviving records describe Henry variously as an ostler, a horsekeeper, a labourer and a coachman.[6]

George White's father, the oldest of five children and another Henry, was born in Honiton in January 1815. Nothing is known of his upbringing or early years, nor is it known why, some time between 1830 and 1843, he chose to leave his family behind and move north to Bristol. Transport may again have exercised its influence, for between 1841 and 1844, the first major railway line out of Bristol was opened.

VIRTUTE ET INDUSTRIA.

A tribute to George White by the Bristol cartoonist F.G. Lewin, echoing the motto of the City of Bristol.

Its route to Exeter bisected the open country between Cullompton and Honiton.[7]

Henry White found employment in Bristol as a painter and decorator and obtained lodgings in Berkeley Crescent. This elegant row of Georgian houses still stands at the corner of Berkeley Square, overlooking shops, offices and University buildings. In those days it looked out beyond the scattered houses of Whiteladies Road, to the open landscape of Tyndall's Park.

Henry was fortunate indeed to live in such a neighbourhood, but his good luck did not end there. Living beside him in the Crescent was another newcomer to Bristol, a lady's maid named Eliza. She was the daughter of John Tippetts, a labourer, and had come to Bristol from the remote Somerset village of Moorlinch.

Henry and Eliza married at St. George's Church, Brandon Hill on August 10th 1843. The painting and decorating business was clearly succeeding, as the young couple were able to move across Tyndall's Park to St. Michael's Buildings, Cotham, a row of pleasant Georgian terraced houses which stood in a little dead-end alley off Paul Street, at the top of St. Michael's Hill.[8]

Cotham in 1843 marked the northernmost edge of the city. There the romantic ramshackle wooden-framed buildings of St. Michael's Hill turned to substantial Georgian terraces and a few Victorian villas, before giving way to the open countryside. The county boundary, dividing Bristol and Gloucestershire, ran almost through Paul Street, up to the turnpike gate on the rural lane to Redland. Cotham House, which featured prominently in George White's later life, stood alone in the fields as the first good house in Gloucestershire.

At No. 2 St. Michael's Buildings, Eliza White gave birth to her children: Henry in 1846, Elizabeth in 1848, Georgina in 1851 and George in 1854. Samuel, the last child, was not born until 1861.[9]

George White almost certainly followed the example of his older brother and sisters and began his education at three or four years old. He attended St. Michael's National School, where the master, Mr. Benjamin Wilson (later described as "the doyen of Bristol school-masters") cared for 190 children.[10]

The school stood behind St. Michael's Church. From below the churchyard the boys could look out across the old city, with its contrasts of wide Georgian squares and narrow ancient streets, its docks, its ships, its rope-walks and its alleys, little changed by the centuries. There they could absorb the sights, the sounds and the smells of commerce.

St. Michael's Buildings, Cotham, Bristol. The terrace on the left of Loxton's sketch of 1912 consisted of eight similar houses, each with its own yard. No. 2, where White was born, was just to the artist's left. It was destroyed by enemy action in World War II. [Avon Library Service]

At fifteen, White left Benjamin Wilson's care and, perhaps with his mother's help, was introduced to the eminent Bristol law partnership of Stanley and Wasbrough, at No.12 Royal Insurance Buildings, Corn Street. There, Mr. John Stanley offered him employment as a junior clerk.[11] Stanley saw ability in the young man and trusted him. He encouraged his self confidence and established in him a firm belief in entrepreneurial freedom, which never left him.

". . . He did not pay me very much," White said in a speech in the last month of his life, "but he was the best friend I ever had. He was the man who made me. . . because he had the sense to let me work out my own salvation. When I had a job given me to do, he expected me to do it − and I did it. . ."[12]

The jobs included looking after the Bristol Law Library, which White did assiduously, avidly reading the books in his care. As a consequence, at the unbelievably youthful age of 16, he was put in overall charge of the firm's bankruptcy work. This was considerable, as a result of the economic depression and the passing of the 1869 Bankruptcy Act. Despite his tender years, he superintended as many as twelve liquidations a time and his experience of how not to run a business became the key to his later success.[13]

White's elder brother Henry reflected on the value of this early education in a letter from Brazil, in 1889. He wrote "Sooner or later the powers of Europe will have to be eating one another up − and when wars and the memory of wars set in, matters may go bad again. However your experience now will guide you to take advantage even of this state of things and you know how to trim your sails so as to take advantage even of stormy weather."[14]

John Stanley's personal forté was in advising businessmen. He knew the men with the power and the money. It had been Stanley and Wasbrough who in 1871, on behalf of a London syndicate, had first proposed a horse-drawn tramway in Bristol's streets, but the City Council had opposed it and in 1873 had built their own line to Redland.[15]

Soon after, when the Council's project failed, Stanley instructed White to assemble a local syndicate and obtain the Parliamentary powers to take the business over.[16] This was not an easy task, as gaining the rights to run a tramway through public streets was more difficult even than gaining the rights to run a railway. If more than one third of the "frontagers", or nearby residents withheld their support, the scheme automatically failed.

White set about conducting the necessary Parliamentary Bills in the teeth of stiff opposition, and was successful, although he was still only

Mr. John Stanley, Bristol solicitor and George White's first employer. "He was the man that made me," White said in later years. His firm continues to flourish, merged with others, as Veale Wasbrough.

Bristol's first tramway service: Maudlin Street, Bristol, 1875. James Clifton Robinson, newly appointed manager, stands proudly on the driver's step in a top hat. [Peter Davey Collection]

eighteen years of age. The Bristol Tramways Company was registered on December 23rd 1874. William Butler, a tar distilling and chemicals magnate, became its first chairman. The board included Henry Gale Gardner, a highly successful wholesaler, and Joseph Wethered, a major coal owner. White was appointed company secretary (a euphemism, as it turned out, for managing director) at the age of twenty and was paid an annual salary of £150.[17]

In the midst of these achievements George White's father died. The presumption must be that George was left to support both his mother and younger brother. His eldest brother Henry, on whom the responsibility should have lain, was unlikely to have contributed much. Henry was a public accountant in partnership with J.W. Young and was a surprisingly well educated man with a good sense of humour, but a dreamer whose grandiose financial schemes regularly turned to ashes. Far from assisting his younger brother, it was not many years before Henry too had become a major drain on George White's income.

Ambitious and wanting more from life than the articles which Mr. Stanley had by now offered, White decided to strike out on his own. He took an office alongside Young and White and Stanley and Wasbrough in Royal Insurance Buildings and set up under the name George White, Stockbrokers and Public Accountants.

1875 and 1876, White's twenty-first and twenty-second years, were of great significance to the young man. His home life, like his business life, underwent considerable change and not even he could possibly have foreseen how, in years to come, the two would blend together to create one of the most successful family empires Bristol had ever seen.

In May 1875 Elizabeth, White's elder sister, married Edward Everard, a young man from Maldon in Essex.[18] Everard had served an apprenticeship as a printer in the City of London, before spending seven years with Hamilton, Adams and Co., leading London printers, publishers and book suppliers.[19] He was a genuinely eccentric man, as the "15th century"[20] ceramic-fronted printing house, which he built in Broad Street Bristol, some twenty five years later, clearly demonstrates. So too does his semi-autobiographical work *A Bristol Printing House, spoken of in several fragments by Edward Everard*, printed entirely in a type-face of his own devising, shortly after the construction of his Broad Street works. However, his curious artistic abilities and his advanced colour and photographic printing were employed in almost all his brother-in-law's subsequent business ventures, and were to prove of inestimable value.

In September, Georgina, White's second sister and a lady's maid, married William George Smith, a butler, in Edinburgh.[21] No one could then have envisaged that of their three sons, two (Henry White Smith and William Verdon Smith) would be launched by their uncle into such significant roles in commerce and would end their days with knighthoods, while the third (Sydney Smith) would become a celebrated early aviator and a colonel in the Royal Flying Corps.

White himself married on June 14th 1876, in St. Barnabas Church, Ashley Road, Bristol.[22] His bride was Caroline Rosina Thomas, daughter of William Thomas, a coach-trimmer, also of Ashley Road. A photograph shows them on their honeymoon at Torquay: two self-conscious young people about to embark on an adventure which would lead not to occasional holidays on the South Coast, but to Nice and Cannes in the Spring and from the faintly absurd clothes of which they were then so proud, to the finest tailors and couturiers of London and Paris.

Their first home was No. 10 Fairlawn, St. Matthew's Road, Cotham. It was (and remains) a small, attractive, mid-Victorian semi-detatched house, not far from the street where White was born.[23] The marriage was a mixture of opposites – a bold extrovert husband and a deeply shy wife – but it worked. Rose supported him with extraordinary courage in his many projects until she died of cancer in November 1915. His despair contributed greatly to his own sudden death only twelve months later.

So little survives of George White's business papers at this date, that it is hard to follow all his interests. But between November 1875, when he appears to have opened his business account with the West of England and South Wales District Bank and December the following year, the funds under his control rose from £25 to £22,123–17–10d. The wages bill for his staff rose from around £43 to £157.[24]

Apart from his tramway interest, he clearly continued to co-operate closely with the firm of Stanley and Wasbrough on all sorts of matters, even though his old mentor, Mr. Stanley, had died in 1878. The work seems to have included letting a wide range of rented property: here, as in bankruptcy work, he saw life in the raw and must have learnt much from the responsibility. "Rogers (at) No. 2," wrote an agent from Bedminster, "This man during the holiday having become drunk & incapable turns to & smashes up all his furniture – now I hear he has broken every pane of glass – and torn down some of the woodwork, doors &c. *What can be done* he is like a madman at present. When sober he earns very good money & soon replaces the furniture again. An early suggestion will greatly oblige."[25]

A small collection of builders' and other maintenance bills survive amongst White's papers, which relate to the properties he controlled.

The printing works in Broad Street, Bristol, built by White's brother-in-law, Edward Everard in 1900. The architect was Henry Williams, the faience decoration was by W.J. Neatby. Everard's name is in an art nouveau typeface which he designed himself.

White's sister Georgina and with her family, c.1900. Standing are her sons Sydney Smith, Henry White Smith and William Verdon Smith, all of whom followed their uncle into the aircraft industry. Seated are her daughters Geraldine and Hilda, who claimed to be the first Englishwomen to fly.

George and Caroline Rose White on their honeymoon in Torquay, 1876.

Some are made out from a firm named White and Son. The bold hand which receipted them is in some ways reminiscent of White's own confident signature. It is just possible therefore that the firm was his father's and that he continued to run it for a brief period after his father's death.[26]

White was elected to the Stock Exchange in 1876, and immediately began to specialise in transport shares. From the first, and despite all his later achievements, he regarded himself primarily as a stock broker. There is little doubt that he quickly became a source of pride and amazement to his fellow citizens, achieving repeated financial coups which had previously been thought possible only within the City of London.[27] His early bank book shows that even at twenty-two years of age, he had financial dealings with William Butler, Stanley and Wasbrough, Wethered, Gardner and two very significant tramway connections, Joseph Kincaid, the highly respected London engineer, and James Clifton Robinson.[28]

Clifton Robinson, who was also to receive a knighthood in later years, was a remarkable man and a leading player in George White's life story. He was six years older than White, having been born in Birkenhead in 1848, the son of a penniless Scottish father and an Irish mother. At fourteen he had wheedled a job as an office boy in the Birkenhead offices of George Francis Train, "that most American of all Americans,"[29] and had fallen hopelessly under his spell. "It seems but yesterday that as a small boy I came under the magnetism of your eloquence," he wrote to Train many years later. "You will I fear hardly remember the minor part I played in the drama during your sojourn in England in the early sixties, or of my career under your auspices in the latter part of that decade, but as you will gather from some of the literary matter which I enclose herewith, I have never ceased to think of and admire your splendid personality. This influence has remained with me through life and any success which has attended my labours has, I am bound to say, been largely due to my early association with your then brilliant career."[30]

Train was indeed larger than life. He was a genius, though always teetering on the edge of sanity. He was an ardent Methodist, an entrepreneur, a trader, a showman and a global traveller. He claimed his eighty-day journey around the world was the inspiration for Jules Verne's novel. As a young man he had nearly become an unwilling rebel President of Tasmania. Later he had become embroiled in the American Civil War. He was caught in the seige of Paris and would have been shot, had he not dramatically wrapped himself in the American flag. He stood as an American Presidential candidate and

19

nearly won. He was largely responsible for building the Canadian Pacific Railway, together with some of the largest ships the world had ever seen and, as he said himself, had served fifteen prison sentences without once committing a crime.[31]

When Clifton Robinson first met him, Train had just fled from London, where he had built a pioneering "street railway" or horse tramway, from Marble Arch to Porchester Terrace, against the greatest possible opposition. Unfortunately, the $4' 8\frac{1}{2}''$ gauge which he had chosen (because that was the standard width of a horse-drawn vehicle) trapped and broke the wheels of passing carriages, and enraged the nobility and gentry. However, his second attempt at Birkenhead in 1860 had succeeded. At the inauguration ceremony on August 30th 1860 (to which all the crowned heads of Europe had been invited, except the King of Naples, of whom Train did not approve), the fourteen-year old Clifton Robinson had squeezed onto the first tram, beside his mentor.[32]

From Train and from later experiences in America, where Train had encouraged him to work and travel, Clifton Robinson had learnt two lessons. The first was how to build a tramway and run traffic. The second was how to use publicity and showmanship to maximum advantage.

In 1875, when he was appointed manager of the horse tramways in Bristol, Robinson found a kindred spirit in George White. The two at once formed what was to become a lifelong friendship and an unbeatable team. From then on in tramway schemes all over Britain, George White ("the man at the other end of the telephone" as Robinson once described him)[33] was to identify the opportunities, provide direction, stability and finance, while Robinson handled the engineering. Flamboyance and showmanship in the spirit of Train was their joint hallmark. "I owe everything to Bristol," Sir Clifton would say, "to Bristol men and Bristol money."[34]

The years from 1875 to 1890 were used by White to consolidate his financial base. They were characterised by relentless hard work, and what was described at the time as his "consummate tact, gentlemanly demeanour and legal acumen."[35] He took no holidays, saying later that "the road to fortune is a long one, and you can only reach it by brains and hard work. If you want to know how I succeeded, it has been by always making up my mind what I intended to do and doing it, and by deciding what I wanted and getting it."[36]

His bread-and-butter income came from stockbroking, but he combined this with an increasing number of important appointments

James Clifton Robinson (1848–1910), engineer and tramway pioneer, drawn by "Spy" in 1909. Robinson played a major rôle in almost all White's tramway projects. He became a lifelong friend and godfather to White's only son. [Bristol Record Office]

George Francis Train (1829–1904) as a United States Presidential candidate in 1869. This eccentric tramway pioneer, entrepreneur and showman exerted a strong influence on Clifton Robinson's early career, and through him, on White's. [Bristol Record Office]

21

emanating from John Stanley's associates. As well as masterminding the massive expansion of Bristol's tramways, in 1881 he became secretary of Gloucester Tramways. He also took on the secretaryship of the Bath Tramways, negotiating the sale of the company in 1884. *Zig-Zag* declared that his advice and aid had been sought by nearly every town in the West and Midlands where trams had been projected. He was in demand in the North too. Appointed liquidator of York Tramways in 1884, he reformed the company with the help of his younger brother Sam and ran it himself for ten successful years from Bristol. "I like the look of the routes very well," wrote Sam on his first investigative visit to the city. "I can see that they lick either Bath or Gloucester into fits. . .but the whole damn thing has been sadly neglected, that's what's the matter. . .It's no good to think of going to one horse anywhere for some time − they are in such a wretched condition, not to say lank, lame and lousy!"[37]

Other transport schemes presented themselves. In 1882, when still only 28 years old, White bought up large blocks of shares in the North Somerset Railway.[38] He soon became a director and also secretary to the promoters of the Bristol and London and South Western Junction Railway, who had designs on the North Somerset's modest tracks.[39] The scheme was an ambitious one, to join central Bristol to Waterloo Station in London. Services would be routed across Somerset, merging with the London and South Western's main line at Grately in Hampshire, thus breaking the London to Bristol monopoly of the Great Western.

A grand new station was planned to span the upper part of the Bristol docks, a space now occupied by the Cenotaph. In the event, the immense power and influence of the Great Western Company prevailed, but in fighting a valiant battle, the young secretary had attracted considerable admiration. "Secretary", as always in George White's case, meant "enabler". The acquisition of shares, negotiations, parliamentary work, publicity and campaigning for all these schemes were centred on his offices, first at 28 Corn Street, by 1885 at 31 Clare Street and finally at 28 Clare Street, known as Clare Street House.

White's personal business ventures sprang from his acute observation of the Stock Exchange, his familiarity and fascination with mass transport, his love of quality and perfection, and from his acute irritation with poor management. Most popular amongst his fellow citizens was his ability to identify the worth in failing companies and turn them into highly successful enterprises, because the benefits spread amongst so many people. The biggest problem he faced was that the sums of money required to achieve these ends were not normally available to a man in his early thirties, who had no collateral security

Clare Street House (28 Clare Street, Bristol), White's headquarters, decorated for the Coronation of George V in June 1911. Bronze plaques on the column bases read: "British & Colonial Aeroplane Company Limited", "George White & Co.", "Western Wagon and Property Company Limited", "Bristol Tramway and Carriage Co.", "Imperial Tramway Company Limited" and "Corris Railway Company". The building was also the registered offices of the Bristol Aeroplane Company. It now houses the Halifax Building Society.

The Severn & Wye & Severn Bridge Railway, bought and sold by White without the knowledge of its directors in 1887. Bristolians and the Bristol press were delighted. [N. Parkhouse]

The Bristol Port Railway, which ran from beneath the Clifton Suspension Bridge to Avonmouth. White negotiated the sale of the company in 1887, in an attempt to break the Great Western monopoly on Bristol Docks. [Port of Bristol Authority]

to offer. White's connections in Bristol commerce however, gave him the entré to the Western Wagon Company.

Western Wagon's primary function was to supply rolling stock for the South Wales railways, but by this date the company had also moved into venture capital and property development. Its chairman was Henry Gale Gardner, wholesaler and friend of John Stanley, who as a board member of the Bristol Tramway Company knew George White well. The company's minute books show that White successfully applied for frequent loans, which he diligently repaid. In 1888 he was appointed secretary to Western Wagon with special responsibility for introducing customers to this growing banking enterprise.[40]

White's personal ventures were as spectacular as those he carried out for his mentors. They were received with delight by both his peers and the press. In the mid-1880s, he quietly turned his attention to the acquisition of shares in the moribund Bristol Port Railway and Pier Company, whose line ran from the foot of the Clifton Suspension Bridge to Avonmouth Docks, a route now partly covered by the Portway. By May 1887 he had become majority shareholder and, calling an extraordinary meeting, was able to convince his fellow shareholders to adopt a scheme which he had devised with the professional assistance of the London engineer, Joseph Kincaid. The target was the Great Western again, but this time centred on its monopoly of Bristol Docks.

The plan was to use the Port and Pier line to link Canon's Marsh, in the Docks, with the Midland Railway, which ran into Avonmouth. Although it proved beyond the little company's means to finance the venture itself, the shareholders found themselves in the happy position of being bought out by an enthusiastic Midland Railway, for the then substantial sum of £97,500.[41]

The Bristol press then revelled in the trouncing of the London Stock Exchange in 1888, a venture enthusiastically described by John Lambert in his *Reminiscences of a Financial Venturer*. Lambert began his career in May & Hassell's timber yard:

which was situate at the extreme end of Bristol Harbour, about a mile from the centre of the city, and one of my duties as a junior clerk was to call at the General Post Office daily to collect from the firm's private box such letters as had arrived by the midday mail. I then used to visit the Commercial Rooms, of which institution the firm were members, for news. One of the senior clerks at the office, Sam Thomas had a brother-in-law, Mr. George White, who was a member of the Bristol Stock Exchange, and I very frequently took notes and messages to him. In 1888

Thomas was in a very depressed state of mind. Owing to some extravagance he had outrun the constable and was being dunned by his creditors, particularly his tailors. So depressed did he become that some of his fellow clerks feared he might be tempted to follow the example of other distraught persons and jump off the Clifton Suspension Bridge.

Suddenly the sun shone through the clouds and his troubles ended in a remarkable way. The famous Brewery of George's & Co. had just been converted into a limited company and a quantity of shares offered to the public. As every businessman in Bristol knew of the soundness of the concern, when the prospectus was issued in February 1888 an extraordinary scramble for shares on the part of the public ensued. It had been intended that the subscription lists should have remained open for a week. The amount asked for was £400,000, but within five hours after the lists had been opened the public had subscribed £6,300,000. At this period a great deal of speculation took place when new shares were issued by a company. Buyers and sellers knew they had plenty of time either to pay for shares bought or deliver shares sold, as they would only have to do so on a date appointed by the Stock Exchange Committee for the special settlement, which would probably be some considerable distance ahead. As George's shares were quoted at a big premium directly the subscription list was closed and continued to rise in price, a number of Stock Exchange speculators in London took the view that they were too high, and sold short, feeling pretty confident that before the settlement day arrived they would be able to buy shares at a lower figure and so cover their commitments and make a profit. What actually happened I will give you in the words of Sam Thomas.

"My brother-in-law, Mr. George White," he said, "realized there would not be any fall in the prices of George's shares as a large portion had been allotted to the licensed trade and others who had bought for permanent investment and would not be likely to sell under any circumstances. He therefore accepted the offers of these London speculators. When the settlement day arrived and these gentlemen had to deliver what they had sold, they found themselves unable to do so, and to bid for shares on the market would only make the holders more anxious to retain what they had got. These 'bears', finding themselves properly cornered, decided to approach Mr. George White, hoping he would be as merciful as he was powerful. He arranged for these defaulters to meet him at his office. He then lectured them on the folly of gambling and allowed them to compound their liabilities on reasonable terms, which they gladly did. This bunch of disillusioned speculators then departed, much relieved of worry and also much relieved of cash, leaving behind them their cheques made payable to Mr. White, amounting in aggregate to over £20,000." Sam Thomas was asked to send his brother-in-law, Mr. George White, particulars of all his debts, which he promptly paid, and my colleague went on his way rejoicing.[42]

In 1890 White staged a similar coup, buying large numbers of shares in Hancocks, the Cardiff brewers[43] and in 1891, at the age of 37, he toppled the entire board of the Taff Vale Railway, in South Wales, by proving mismanagement against them.[44] But his greatest success of the period, in the eyes of the press at least, was his steady acquisition of shares in the failing Severn and Wye and Severn Bridge Railway, so that by mid-1893 he had achieved control. On the strength of it, he travelled to Paddington where he privately negotiated terms for a sale to the Great Western and Midland, jointly. Next he went to Gloucester, where he called the board together. To the astonishment of the directors, he laid out the sale cut and dried before them, which they found they had no choice but to accept. Characteristically he was said to have obtained generous pensions for all of them. Nevertheless the mention of his name in boardrooms thereafter was said to have struck terror into the hearts of mediocre businessmen.[45]

The mid and late 1890s were a period of consolidation and of particular achievement in tramways. In 1892, White acquired a majority shareholding in the failing Imperial Tramways, and removed the old directors and took over as chairman. His old friend Clifton Robinson became managing director and together they were able to use the company to take control of businesses throughout Britain. The Imperial already owned networks in Reading, Dublin and Middlesbrough. Thrown in was the little Corris Railway in the slate quarries of mid-Wales, whose diminutive steam trains still operate on the neighbouring Tallyllyn track.[46]

In early 1894, White was appointed receiver of the collapsed Metropolitan Tramways Company in London, which owned tracks in Hammersmith and Shepherd's Bush. Before the year was out, he relaunched it as London United Tramways.[47] Again he took the chair himself and appointed Clifton Robinson managing director and engineer. His younger brother Sam, a mathematical genius, joined the board, as did his brother-in-law Edward Everard. His nephew, William Verdon Smith became company secretary. Like all his other concerns, the L.U.T. became a true Victorian family business.

It is impossible to describe briefly the expansion they achieved in all the cities their tramways served, but using every ounce of publicity they could muster, including their own newspapers like the *Chiswick Tramway News*,[48] they fought reticent councils and unwilling frontagers, campaigned for pro-tramway councillors at elections, negotiated parliamentary bills, altered streets and relaid highways.

> "We to-day's procession leading; we, the route for travel clearing,
> Pioneers! O Pioneers!"

wrote Clifton Robinson.[49] They were engineering a social revolution. For the first time, inner-city dwellers in the five cities where they operated could move out from the central slums to better and cheaper housing in the suburbs. The age of the commuter had begun.

Always ready to adopt the latest advances, Robinson and White set about importing American technology to Bristol. On October 14th 1895 George White, now officially recognised as managing director of the Bristol Tramways, opened the first electric tramway service in Britain, running from Kingswood to St. George. And how else should he and Robinson launch it, but with a celebration worthy of George Francis Train? As thousands thronged the streets, the managing director stood silk-hatted on the top deck of the leading tram. Clifton Robinson was at the controls of the second. The Royal Artillery Band was engaged to accompany the ceremony and a banquet was thrown for the guests. Free rides were arranged for shareholders and a "meat dinner" was staged for 1,200 deserving poor, amounting to 1,200lbs of meat, 280lbs of cake, 1,250 bread rolls, 900 buns, 70lbs of sugar and 130 gallons of milk and tea. Similar technical advances were made on lines throughout England with massive improvements in services.[50]

To celebrate the inauguration of the capital's first commercial electric tram service in July 1901, the largest of the London United car-sheds was transformed into a banqueting hall. Present were George White and Clifton Robinson, the chairman and managing director. Their guests included the Marquess of Lansdowne, the Earl Grey, the Earl of Rosse, the Lord Herries, The Lord Rothschild, the Lord Revelstoke, four other peers, eight knights (including Sir Hiram Maxim), five members of Parliament and a multitude of bankers, lawyers and prominent citizens. Even Mr. J. Pierpont Morgan, son of the world-famous American railway magnate was there. George Francis Train would have advocated nothing less. In the Loyal Toast,

Showmanship worthy of G.F. Train. The inauguration of the first conventional electric tramway service in Britain, at Old Market, Bristol in October 1895. White, top-hatted, stands on the first tram. [Peter Davey]

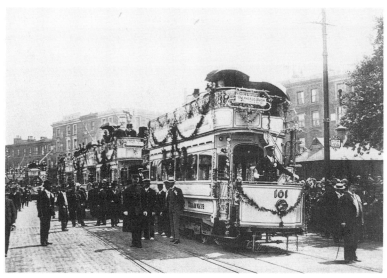

"One of the greatest engines of social reform." The launch of London's first conventional electric tramway service in 1901. Clifton Robinson adopts a Chaplinesque stance ahead of the first flower-decked tram.

High Road, Chiswick. The brand new Central Power House and Car Sheds on the opening day of London United Electric Tramways, 1901. Wags claimed "L.U.E.T." was Latin for "let there be light".

Art, technology and high quality combine. The Central Power House switchboard, London United Tramways, 1901. Photographs show a similar switchboard had been built for Bristol Tramways, at the Counterslip Power Station.

White referred to the King's "great sympathy with the movement in which we are interested today" because "working men would be able to secure not merely healthier but cheaper houses" in the suburbs. Arthur J. Balfour M.P., leader of the House of Commons, enthusiastically followed this theme, believing that the enterprise was "one of the greatest engines of social reform and of social amelioration which it has been the privilege of any great corporation to start."[51] Remarkable new tramway depots had been constructed and the latest in power generating stations had been built. As always with George White, no corners had been cut and nothing was spared in the quest for perfection.[52]

In his spare time, White campaigned tirelessly for the Conservative Party in Bristol and Bath. Although he later turned down the safe Conservative seat of Bristol West (it was said that nothing less than a cabinet seat would interest him), in 1890 he did stand for the Bristol Ward of the city council and was elected. He dropped local politics soon after, but not before he had defeated the council's plan to replace the drawbridge over the city docks near the Hippodrome with a bascule or lifting bridge. His victory as chairman of the "Fixed Bridge Scheme" was celebrated in 1892 by the presentation of a silver jardinière by his fellow committee members. The citation recorded "his indomitable energy and determination in bringing the movement to a successful issue."[53]

George White was a committed workaholic and an inveterate smoker of cigars, which by now he bought from leading dealers in New Bond Street, in London, and his health was bound to suffer. The first suggestion of a major problem appears in an eye-witness description of the closing moments of a financial coup which he masterminded in 1902.[54] It related to the construction of the London tube-train system, which with recent advances in electrical technology had become a lucrative possibility. Recognising this, a number of syndicates had begun to form to compete for the necessary Acts of Parliament. George White and Clifton Robinson were among them, through an offshoot of London United Electric Tramways (as their company was now called), called the London United Electric Railways Company. They were up against the Titans however, because amongst the opposition were the rival American railway magnates, J. Pierpont Morgan and Charles Tyson Yerkes, who had arrived in London, each confident of gaining overall control.

The White/Robinson scheme to run lines beneath the whole of western London (even between what Robinson had described the Scylla of the Albert Hall and the Charybdis of the Albert Memorial),[55] clashed with Pierpont Morgan's and Charles Yerkes' even greater ambitions in the same area. It soon became obvious that to win parliamentary approval, a partnership with one or other opposition group was necessary.

An arrangement was negotiated in principle with Morgan, in which his company was to provide capital of £7,690,000 and George White, through L.U.E.R., £3,690,000.[56] From the start the relationship was an uneasy one, since Morgan had little time for those he considered bit-part players in his great schemes. George White, who was equally accustomed to controlling his own destiny, resented Morgan's attitude and disliked his methods. He made it clear that he would withdraw his personal investment if matters did not improve. It was not until the Bill had passed through the Lords and was in its final stages in the Commons, however, that matters finally boiled over. Without further discussion, White entered negotiations with Speyer Brothers of Lothbury, bankers acting for Yerkes. Within twenty-four hours he had sold them his 80 per cent interest in London United Electric Tramways, delivering victory to the opposition. A torrent of abuse followed from Morgan supporters and from those who believed that the Americans had wilfully wasted parliamentary time. Sir Lewis McIver, Chairman of the Commons Select Committee on the Bills, described it as "a Stock Exchange Ramp" and "a game in which it was proposed to make the London roads pawns on the chequer board of Wall Street".[57]

The eye witness, who was present when White informed the Parliamentary Committee of his actions, described the scene. Morgan's leading counsel lost his temper. Sir Clinton Dawkins, Morgan's English representative, sank forward with his head in his hands. George White went out into the corridor and fainted. This was almost certainly an early symptom of syncope, or loss of consciousness through failing blood pressure which was eventually to kill him, but it was also one of the reasons that his doctors insisted that he should take regular breaks in the South of France, the significance of which will become apparent later.[58]

White's wife Caroline Rose bore him two children: Daisy May, born in 1877 and George Stanley, named after old Mr. Stanley the solicitor, in 1882. As White's successes grew, so too did his houses. From No. 10 Fairlawn, the little house in St. Matthew's Road Cotham, George and Caroline White moved first to a house near the Tramway Depot at Filton, which they also called Fairlawn.[59] They then moved to No. 94 Redland Road, which they called Fairlawn again: there Stanley was born.[60] Their next move was

George and Caroline White on holiday at Tenby, with their children (George) Stanley and Daisy, c.1886.

"An uncommon nice place." Cotham House, Bristol, a fine Georgian house much altered in the 19th century, was White's home from 1889–1915.

The drawing room with festive decorations. Floral swags and archway contain what may have been the first domestic 'fairy' lights in Bristol, reflecting White's involvement in pioneering electrical technology.

to Stapleton, but 1889 must have seen a dream realised, for the family moved back to Cotham, but not to the dead-end alley off Paul Street, nor to the more elegant but modest St. Matthew's Road, but to the big house, Cotham House, on the crest of the hill.[61] Henry White (who under continuing financial pressure had by then decamped to Brazil) wrote discouragingly from Sao Paulo "I can sometimes picture you to myself at Cotham House – it must be an uncommon nice place and one of the few in its class remaining, but someday it will get too dear to live in – and you will have to cut it up."[62]

Two years later, however, White's tax return showed four male servants, three carriages with four or more wheels, one carriage with two wheels and five dogs.[63] A vet's bill of the same period even suggests the presence of a house-cow within his boundaries.[64] Between then and 1905 White spent a fortune on refitting his house, using the architect George Oatley (later Sir George), whose fame today rests largely on the great Bristol University Tower which he designed some years later for the Wills family.

Joinery for Cotham House was commissioned from the Bath Cabinet Makers, through Messrs. Smith of St. Augustine's Parade. It cost £8,000 to make and £1,000 to instal. Smiths also supplied much of the furniture and interior decoration.[65] The entrance hall was of the highest quality, more akin to a great ocean liner than a house in Cotham, but like the other rooms, it reflected the meticulous nature of its owner. By 1904 the contents and works of art were valued at £60,000.[66] Furnishing was mostly modern (because he wanted the latest and he wanted perfection), but in a "period" style. This was set off with small antiques.

Amongst other dealers he patronised was J.P. Way of Park Street, Bristol. In 1956, Way's son remembered:

It was about this time (c. 1910) that Sir George White first came in to our shop. He was indeed the grand old man of Bristol, and his business acumen as well as his generosity had done much for the city. His name, I'm sure will never be forgotten there. . . He was a fine, good-looking man, with a well-built upright figure and a white military-looking moustache. On that first visit he bought, amongst other things, some fine porcelain vases which he wanted us to send to various friends for Christmas presents. When he left, my father said importantly, "I will book this myself," and I can still see him as he adjusted his pince-nez, opened the day book and wrote in his beautiful bold handwriting, "Sir George White, Bart." I think it made him feel that now he was really established.

On another occasion Sir George noticed a pair of Empire

Cotham House garden, 1907. George and Caroline White (centre), with the veterans of the Crimean War and the Indian Mutiny. The towering military figure to their right is General Lord Methuen.

period ormolu and bronze candlesticks, from the cut-glass drip pans of which hung icicle-shaped drops. "That's just what I want," he said, pointing to them, "if I buy them, I presume you can make each drop hang evenly?" he asked.[67]

He bought no Old Masters, preferring what he considered the best of modern art. In Caroline Rose's drawing room hung pictures by Birket Foster, Sir John Gilbert, Copley Fielding and Haag.[68] In the window bay he installed Barias' then famous statue of *Victory*, which he had bought for 7,000 francs from Susse Frères showroom in Paris in June 1904.[69] The inner hall contained the works of Gérome and Rosa Bonheur. In the dining room hung pictures by Leighton, Leader, Verboeckhoven and the *pièce de résistance* in contemporary eyes, symbolic because White was so often compared to the Emperor, Edward Détaille's *Napoleon in Egypt*.[70]

Perhaps understandably for a self made man, White took especial pleasure in fine jewellery. His own collection and his wife's (especially the perfectly matched pearls which she so often wore around her neck) caused a sensation when they were auctioned to pay death duties in 1917.[71] The best went to America. Photographs and surviving receipts show that he assembled a good collection of gold boxes and *objets d'art* too. When Carl Fabergé, jeweller to the Czar opened his celebrated shop in London, White acquired a group of hardstone animals and a sublime gold and enamel photograph frame, to contain his own portrait. He also purchased a "magot", or articulated figure of a Chinese god, cut from green Siberian jade and decorated with rubies, pearls and diamonds. They were a quality he adored.

Entertaining at Cotham was as perfectly arranged as the house itself. The Bristol papers delighted in describing the receptions and garden parties held there for social and charitable purposes. The lunch for the Veterans of the Crimean and Indian Mutiny Campaigns on June 22nd 1907 was among the most poignant. "The Bristol Veterans' Association has a membership of 91, and of these no fewer than 81 were on parade, quite a record number when it is remembered that the ages of the men range from 70 to 84. . . . it was a pathetic sight to see these old men – some blind, others only just able to totter along – slowly advancing in file across the lawn to the strains of 'The Boys of the Old Brigade'."

Following lunch, the visitors were addressed by General Lord Methuen and by White, who it must be remembered was only seven months old when some of his guests were witnessing the horrendous events at Balaclava. "The old men then wandered round the grounds, or sat under trees enjoying a quiet smoke and listening to the band." After tea, Caroline Rose presented each with "a souvenir of his visit in the shape of a tin of tobacco and a pipe, enclosed in a leather case, upon which was stamped 'C. and I.M.V.A. With Lady White's best wishes'. The men were then driven back to headquarters in high spirits."[72]

Nothing, though, compared with the lavish reception which followed the marriage of White's daughter, Daisy in 1902. "Although the residence is a spacious habitation, there was not a room large enough to accommodate so many guests. . . so the bride's father had an annexe added. The temporary structure, which was attached to the drawing-room, by which it was reached, was 50 feet square and 14 feet high. It was most luxuriously decorated, furnished, upholstered and adorned with flowers and foliage plants. The walls were coloured a delicate green. Above was an exquisite frieze in charming shades of green and terra cotta, and the ceiling was covered with a specially-chosen paper to harmonise with the walls and frieze. The apartment was divided by a beam, supported by substantial Corinthian columns, the bases of which were arranged in the form of electric heating chambers, enclosed in copper panels, having attractive perforated patterns. The pillars and woodwork were enamelled in white. On the left hand side, facing the window, was an artistic mantelpiece and overmantle in ivory white, with copper fireplace, ornamented at the sides with olive-green Minton tiles. The upper panel of the overmantel consisted of a bronze in relief, representing the 'Road to Tournay', and the panel underneath was filled with a Venetian mirror. The furnishing was very handsome. The carpets were of terra cotta shades; the curtains were Velours velvet, of rich shades; and heavy draperies in each bay harmonised with the surroundings. The windows were draped with festoon blinds of ivory silk, and on each side there were curtains of embroidered satin. A good deal of the furniture, which was designed and made specially, was of sycamore, a lovely cool grey-green colour, and beautifully inlaid with many choice woods, the lounges and settees being upholstered in green silk and Genoa velvet. The walls were adorned chiefly with more than thirty five paintings, presented to the bride by an uncle. The illumination was effected by numerous French electroliers of antique brass, suspended from the ceiling and attached to the walls in the form of brackets, the electric lights being in the shape of imitation candles, softened with old gold silk shades.

"Foliage plants of the choicest kinds were employed in the embellishment of the reception pavilion. . . greatest of all the attractions of the apartment was a floral bell, suspended from the ceiling near the bay window. It measured about 12 feet in circumference, and was about four feet in length. It was thus built up. Around the rim were choice orchids. Then came a broad band of lilies of the valley. Next a wonderful ring of yellow daffodils. The body of the bell was constructed of white chrysanthemums. At the shoulder was another ring of daffodils: over it was a scroll work of violets, on a ground of gardenias and white roses; and a single band of daffodils surmounted the whole of the floral structure. The crown of the bell consisted entirely of Roman hyacinths. On one side of the body was a medallion of yellow satin, bordered with roses, the centre being filled with the monogram 'E D' (Ernest, Daisy), in Parma violets. Inside the bell there was a lining of white ivory silk, with a top of chiffon, through which many electric lamps cast their rays. Upon the silk were trailings of asparagus ferns, a border of lilies of the valley, and a chain work of Parma violets, tied with true lovers knots with ribbon to match. The tongue of the bell was covered with lillium lancifolium. The floral embellishments of the improvised drawing room were extended throughout the house. . ." and so the description continued, marvelling that all this should be so − on the third day of December. Even the garden had been entirely replanted "with blooms to represent late autumn", the carriageway had been covered with an awning of scarlet and white drapery, "incandescent lights, with artistic shades, were suspended from the roof", while borders of bamboo and palms had been planted outdoors to complete the picture.[73]

If all this was not satisfaction enough for a 'self-made' man, in June 1904 White received a personal letter from the Prime Minister A.J. Balfour, with whom he had been acquainted for some time. It informed him of the "King's intention to create him a baronet of the United Kingdom" in the birthday honours. "Believe me," wrote White to Balfour "it will always be a treasured remembrance to know that *you* should have deemed me worthy of your recommendation to the King's favour and I beg you to accept my very warmest thanks for this added pleasure."[74] The letter was perhaps not unexpected in the family. Henry White, a wistful observer of his native city from his self-imposed exile in Brazil, had written home scornfully on the subject of honours on a number of occasions. In 1889 he observed that "the crop of 'belted knights' grows − it is many a long day since Bristol had three of them. . . honours seem to be getting cheaper and if they go on so − won't be worth having." In 1890 he noted the death of Alderman James Ford: "who now will help the ambitious ones who want knighthoods? All such Humbug!"[75]

By 1902, however, he had changed his views. "It does one good," he wrote "to read how thoroughly you have won your place in the roll of benefactors in contributing to solve the difficult questions of the social and housing conditions of the masses. If at the Coronation your name is not included in the "list of honours" I don't think his most gracious (majesty) Edward 7th will have done what he ought to do. . . I really think if you care to take it that you ought to get a Baronetcy."[76] Though no record of the precise reason for Balfour's recommendation seems to have survived, the *Financial News* later noted that White "regarded it rather as a recognition of the services rendered to his native city, to which he was intensely attached, than to his wider public work."[77]

The official registration of White's new armorial bearings turned into a characteristic battle of wills between White and W.A. Lindsay, Windsor Herald. Addressing Sir George most pointedly as George White Esq., Lindsay wrote "the picture you have sent does not seem capable of being 'blazoned', that is described in heraldic language. The *theory* is that when a combatant enters a tournament. . . his shield should be proclaimed by the herald. I think the herald would in this case be put to such difficulty that the combatant would have to wait at the entrance to the lists for some hours. . . Forgive me again for impressing on you that whether there has been anything gazetted or not, you cannot *be* a Baronet till the arms and pedigree are *certified* by the College."[78] Lindsay's original sketch offered a shield dominated by pheasants: the design that emerged could not have been more different. The principal charge is a 'lymphad' or ship against a blue sea, reflecting the arms of the City of Bristol and celebrating its spirit of exploration and commerce. Above are two roses, in honour of Caroline Rose, his wife. The crest is a fiery beacon, hung with a sail: again "charged with a rose". In outline it reflects the crest of the Society of Merchant Venturers, whose bold seafaring past was seen at the turn of the century as the very essence of all that made Bristol great. In substance it symbolised the foresight for which White was so often celebrated. The motto, which he composed himself, reads "Ever Watchful".

Perhaps it was the sense of having "arrived" in society that turned the new baronet hugely to philanthropy. Not that the idea was new to him, for as the *Bristol Magpie* had noted on March 8th 1890 "on the occasion of the great flood in Bristol, he was the man who wrote the first letter suggesting the starting of a Mayor's Relief Fund, and . . . headed the subscription list with a three figure sum before anyone else had moved." He had come to be recognised as a champion of the people, the paper said, noting his recent rescue of the Bristol Benevolent Institution. "Surely it may be said of him," it concluded, "as it was said of Cimon of Greece, that he gets his riches to use them, and so uses them as to be honoured on their account."

40

In 1898, White and his younger brother Samuel, whose exceptional numerical skills George now employed in all his ventures, set up a free pension scheme for the Bristol Tramway workers. They shared the cost of £2,000.[79] In 1903, having been by now elected President of the Bristol Stock Exchange, White commissioned the architect Henry Williams to design new premises worthy of the city and on July 30th 1903, presented the finished exchange in St. Nicholas Street to its members.[80] It still stands, furnished in the style of Cotham House.

In 1904, as had become his custom, he took Caroline Rose to the South of France. There he was reportedly shocked to find that a project to commemorate the late Queen Victoria's long association with the French Riviera had collapsed in ignominy. The idea had been to build a memorial hospital at Mount Boron, between Nice and Cannes, but as the building grew, Sir Blundell Maple who had promised to finance the final stages, died. The executors of his estate backed out of his commitment. "In doubt as to the prospects of success, subscribers ceased to come forward, and the unfinished structure and its promoters became the object of satirical comment, undeserved but hardly unnatural."[81] White stepped in at once with the necessary £3,000 and in due course became its President. He and Caroline Rose were not only present at its opening in 1906 by Queen Victoria's daughter, H.R.H. Princess Christian of Schleswig-Holstein, but took a personal and loving interest in its day-to-day progress, until their own deaths in 1915 and 1916. "Last March H.R.H. Princess Christian declared the new hospital to be open to the public. This important event was solemnized by the Bishop of Gibraltar and his clergy and was witnessed by as smart a crowd as the Riviera has ever seen. . . for in truth this hospital is one of the most perfect of its kind to be found anywhere . . . and assuredly everyone will agree with the writer that of all the many memorials to Queen Victoria, none is more perfect or more worthy of her undying memory," enthused a reporter on the *Menton and Monte Carlo News*.[82]

But White's greatest enthusiasm (apart from the numerous donations he gave every day) was the Bristol Royal Infirmary. It was, after all, almost within sight of his birthplace. When he was elected President and Treasurer on May 5th 1904, it was crippled with debts amounting to £15,552.[83] With the aid of the "extraordinary magnetic influence" he was said to have had over "all that were brought into contact with him,"[84] he at once set about its relief, planning an event billed as the greatest entertainment Bristol had ever seen. It was to be a glittering Carnival, held in the Bristol Zoological Gardens, running from June 26th to July 1st 1905. "His Highness though unable to

"It may be safely said that. . . no other city in the Empire has a stock exchange in such perfect taste and completeness," said the *Financial News*. White commissioned the building and presented it for Bristol's use in 1903. It is shown here in 1935, decorated for the Silver Jubilee of George V.

"None more perfect or worthy." The Queen Victoria Memorial Hospital, Nice, at its opening in 1906 by H.R.H. Princess Christian of Schleswig-Holstein. In World War II, the building was stripped of its contents and destroyed by occupying forces. Now known as the British American Hospital, its work continues on another site.

attend the fête heartily sympathises with your public spirited efforts" wrote the Prince of Wales's secretary. Included in the programme were eight performances a day in two specially built temporary theatres, "The Clifton Coliseum" and "The Clifton Hippodrome", by a galaxy of popular performers such as Wilkie Bard, the comedian, Louie Freear the comedienne and no less a celebrity than "the World's Champion Sand Dancer". Two orchestras and two bands performed non-stop outdoor concerts, dozens of stalls were erected, including one under the command of Caroline Rose, sideshows and other novelties were provided and even trips in new-fangled private motor cars were arranged.[86] Great importance was attached to spectacular presentation and White once again tapped the artistic skills of his brother-in-law. "There are few places which lend themselves to illuminations better than the Gardens," opined the *Bristol Magpie*, "and the scheme of colouring which Mr. E. Everard has arranged is a scene worthy of the Arabian Nights."[87]

Nationwide publicity was generated on a scale worthy of George Francis Train, by controversy over a planned raffle of works of art, which came dangerously close to bending the law on lotteries, which were then illegal. "Allow me to say I think you will raise a hornet's nest round you if you allow the Scheme for the Infirmary Debt to continue," thundered Edward Robinson from "The Towers", Sneyd Park, Bristol.[88] No doubt White knew that when he pressed ahead.

The Dean of Bristol at once renounced all connection with the Infirmary. The Bishop resigned as patron and rallied 145 clergymen to write to the press. Supported by the Bishop of Hereford, he raised the matter in the House of Lords. "I am very sorry that the Bishop intends to call the attention of the House of Lords on Monday to the Bristol Art Union Drawings. I shall be pleased to attend the House on that day, but fear I can do very little good as I expect the Bishop will merely make a statement which will be replied to by someone representing the Board of Trade and there the matter will end," wrote a laconic Duke of Beaufort to White.[89] And ended it was, by the Duke of Marlborough and the Foreign Secretary, Lord Lansdowne who spoke somewhat unwillingly for the Government. The newspapers, however, revelled in it and day after day lampooned the Bishop and Dean for their mean-mindedness. The Carnival was a triumph, raising £4,023, which Samuel White promptly doubled. White himself then added a further £7,514, wiping out the Infirmary debt at a stroke.[90]

For sure as two and one makes three,
The name of White's a guarantee

"Charity Universal No. 2": the second in a series of cartoons in the *Bristol Magpie*, lampooning the Bishop's attempt in the House of Lords, to stop White's fundraising raffle for the new Infirmary. White is shown in a top hat, his brother Samuel in a bowler. [Avon Library Service]

White lays the foundation stone of the new hospital extension in March 1911. He was described as Bristol Infirmary's "second founder".

44

That things are done most thoroughly
As mortal man can do. . .

wrote a versifier for the *Magpie*.[91]

White was not satisfied with breaking even, and on July 11th 1905, he launched an appeal for £50,000 to enable the Infirmary to be brought up to date and extended. Within six months £41,132 had been pledged, but there the appeal began to stick.[92] George and Samuel White made up the difference from their own pockets and the planning of an extension of the most advanced sort was undertaken. The architect chosen was Charles Holden (1875–1960). The Infirmary has since been described as "one of the most important buildings in the history of modern architecture."[93]

On March 14th 1911, White laid its foundation stone, which – until February 1995 [see page viii] – was his only public memorial in Bristol. The Edward VII Memorial Infirmary was declared open on June 28th 1912 by King George V and Queen Mary, in a day of pageantry and splendour. The declaration, made with White proudly looking on, was greeted with a flourish of trumpets and the ringing of church bells throughout the city.[94] Parties were staged in all the public parks, as Bristolians turned out in their thousands to celebrate their good fortune. That evening, while "Lady White and party visited Pringle's Picture House at Zetland Road. . .and were much interested in the films taken in the afternoon, of the ceremony at the Infirmary", a 'complimentary and congratulatory dinner' was held for the hospital's president. In his speech White paused briefly to reflect on his triumph, but was characteristically more concerned with the future. "The building itself is noble," he said, "let us see that the work carried on inside it is of a similar character."[95]

White had meanwhile established a branch of the Red Cross in Bristol and was serving as its treasurer. Caroline Rose served as its vice president. J.H. Howell later "remembered well the inaugural meeting at the Victoria Rooms, when many people thought Sir George was an unnecessary alarmist, but he looked ahead and realised how such an organisation would be needed in the dark days which had now come upon us."[96]

The King Edward Memorial Building became "Bristol's Red Cross Hospital" on the outbreak of the First World War (constituting half of the 2nd Southern General Hospital), and treated 20,000 sick and wounded soldiers as in-patients and 50,000 as out-patients.[97]

It is sad, perhaps, that the Samuel White and Eliza White Wards, named after his brother and his mother, no longer commemorate them, or remind the city of this fragment of its history.[98]

45

June 28th 1912. George V and Queen Mary declare the Edward VII Memorial Hospital open. "I know everything there will be of the best and latest," the King said privately to White, who here stands to his right.

"One of the most important buildings in the history of modern architecture". The hospital shown on a contemporary postcard, with the King, Queen and White inset above.

George White had sold out his business interests in London in 1902, but now he was busier than ever. Stockbroking from Bristol (through George White and Co.), banking and property development (through the Western Wagon Company, which he now chaired) and tramway extensions (he was chairman of both Imperial Tramways and Bristol Tramways) occupied much of his time. Political campaigning still concerned him greatly. He served as a magistrate. He became president of the Bristol Dolphin Society and raised more than £2,000 for their charitable work. He served on the Council of Bristol University, receiving an honorary doctorate of law in 1912. The social aspects of the enlightened "garden suburb" development which the Western Wagon Company was undertaking at Filton interested him greatly. He had not entirely lost his enthusiasm for restructuring railway systems either. Indeed his most audacious scheme of all, devised in 1910 in conjunction with the Marquis of Bute, was to merge the Taff Vale Railway in South Wales, with the Rhymney Railway and the Cardiff Railway. Success would have brought him a personal commission of £53,000 and cornered 40 per cent of the Welsh steam coal carrying market, but the plan failed, through a single vote in the House of Commons.[99] White then became a coal-owner himself, by buying into the Main Colliery, near Neath, in 1908. He joined the board with his brother Sam in 1909 and became chairman in 1910. His overwhelming concern in the decade 1900 to 1910, however, was to keep one step ahead technologically.

White had, with Clifton Robinson, opened the first commercial electric tramway service in England. Now he turned to the internal combustion engine. It is not known when he first obtained a car, but Sam White ordered a Mercedes in 1902[100] and George White bought his son Stanley a Panhard-Levassor for his twenty-first birthday in 1903.[101] Both cars still survive. Such a means of transport quickly commended itself to the family, for White himself was soon the owner of a fleet of cars, many of which he seems to have obtained through the Paris motor dealer, Émile Stern of 17 Rue Montaigne.[102] There were a number of different makes, including a large Mercedes and after 1913 a pair of Rolls-Royce "Silver Ghosts", but perhaps significantly in the mid-decade, he purchased at least two Léon Bollées.

It had been no surprise therefore when at some time around the end of 1904, he made the decision to invest in motor buses. He told the shareholders of the Bristol Tramway and Carriage Company that he knew such vehicles were not yet commercially viable, but that he proposed to keep ahead by running them experimentally on the horse bus routes, so that he could assess them and iron out their problems.[104] The first Thorneycroft bus route from the Bristol Victoria Rooms to the Clifton Suspension bridge was so successful that soon motor buses were extending the Bristol Tramway system as far north as Berkeley and as far east as Newton St. Loe, outside Bath. In May 1908 he took the bold step of entering industry, by setting up a production line at Filton to manufacture commercial vehicles himself.[105] Nearly 40 chassis with Bristol "X" type petrol engines were produced, before he moved production to larger premises in Brislington in 1912. The early versions had brass radiators, wooden wheels, solid tyres, and chain drive.[106]

In September 1908, he introduced the motor taxi to Bristol.[107] The first two experimental Charrons arrived from Paris, again almost certainly from Émile Stern. Nothing of course was done on a small scale. By 1914, his Bristol company alone was running 17 tramway services, 15 omnibus services, 169 tramcars, 44 buses, 29 charabancs and 124 taxis. Services included hotel buses, private car hire, lorry hire to individual companies (including the Royal Mail), vans, charabanc tours and hearses.[108] 1912 saw the addition of the Clifton Rocks Railway to his empire. In 1912 and 1913 he opened branches of his Bristol company in Cheltenham and Gloucester, in addition to the taxi service which had been running in Bath since 1909.[109]

Having kept ahead on land, White then turned his attention to the air. The history books have it that in 1909, on one of the many holidays he took in the South of France to alleviate his increasing health problems, he saw some Frenchmen flying and underwent an instant conversion to aviation. Unconsidered action of this kind was not his style. In all transport forms, he had watched development, waited until it had reached the edge of viability and then used his own particular talents to put it to practical use.

In 1904, when George and Samuel White had launched the second phase of their pension scheme for tramway employees with large personal donations, the Bristol papers had given them extensive coverage. White's own copy of the *Bristol Daily Mercury* for February 17th still survives in Bristol Record Office. Directly opposite the full page report of his speech (which he surely must have noted with pleasure), is a small line drawing of an aircraft. The short article below relates how two brothers named Wright, from Dayton, Ohio not only claimed to have flown a heavier than air device, but far more significantly for a transport pioneer such as George White, to have successfully steered it in flight. If White did experience a sudden conversion to the possibilities of aerial navigation, this frail 1904 newspaper must surely have been the cause of it.

36 Tyndall's Park Road, Bristol, lent by Caroline White to the Bristol Red Cross as its wartime headquarters. White furnished Clare Chambers (next to Clare Street House), and made it available to the Red Cross as a publicity and financial centre. He paid all Branch staff salaries himself.

White enters industry. The Bristol C40 chassis, with a 16-seat single-deck bus body, was the first commercial vehicle to emerge from the Filton works in May 1908. It was powered by a Bristol X-type petrol engine with chain drive. Commercial vehicle production moved to Brislington in October 1912, where Bristol lorries and buses continued to be made until 1983. [M. Tozer]

White's health problems led him to take frequent holidays in the fashionable resorts of the South of France, especially Nice and Cannes. Using two Rolls-Royce 'silver-ghosts', he and his wife made excursions into Italy and Spain.

From that moment onwards the evidence suggests that he kept in constant touch with those who themselves had contact with aviation. Émile Stern, the Parisian motor dealer may well have been the lynch pin. Stern had been intimately involved in arranging the purchase of a Léon Bollée for White in 1908, at exactly the same time as Bollée and Wilbur Wright were assembling and demonstrating the latest Wright Flyer at Bollée's factory at Le Mans.[110] Given the volume of motor business Stern was conducting with George White's multifarious concerns, it seems unlikely that he would not have passed on news of the mechanical marvels and aeronautical triumphs that were taking place around him. It seems no coincidence either, that when White did found his own aircraft works at Filton, he appointed Stern as his agent in the French capital.

It seems to have been at Pau in 1909, where Wright was flying again, that White made his decision.[111] Flying machines had reached that critical point in their development which appealed to his business sense. In his now famous speech to the Tramway shareholders of February 1910, he summed up his philosophy. "I may tell you that for some time past my brother and I have been directing our attention to the subject of aviation, which is one hardly yet ripe for practical indication by such a company as The Bristol Tramways Company, but yet seems to offer promise of development at no distant date; so much so that we have determined personally to take the risks and expense of the endeavour to develop the science from the spectacular and commercial or manufacturing point of view." He envisaged demonstrations in the spirit of G.F. Train, with accommodation for 100,000 spectators (and consequent profit to the tramways), but it was the *Western Daily Press* reporter who reached the heart of the matter. "The thoughts of these Bristolians," he wrote, "anticipate the time when flying machines will be so perfected that they will be reckoned among the methods of travel."[112]

The Bristol Aeroplane Company, the Bristol Aviation Company, the British and Colonial Aeroplane Company, and the British and Colonial Aviation Company were carefully founded on the same day, to give White maximum flexibility. So that he would not prejudice any application to use the name 'Bristol' as a registered trade mark, he chose to begin trading as the 'British and Colonial'.[113] It is undoubtedly his determination to name his craft after his beloved native city and not after himself, that subsequently robbed him of the lasting fame of A.V. Roe, Sopwith, the Short Brothers, C.S. Rolls and the other contemporary pioneers whose products soon made them household names.

Capital was subscribed by White himself, his brother Samuel and his

51

"The Aerostat." An illustration from White's own copy of the *Bristol Daily Mercury* (February 17th 1904), which reported that "two young men of Dayton, Ohio, have constructed a machine which. . . easily flew more than three miles." [Bristol Record Office]

The moment of decision. This flight by Wilbur Wright at Pau (1909) was said to have been witnessed by White. If so, it almost certainly persuaded him that aeronautics were now sufficiently advanced for him to turn to the development of air travel himself. [Science Museum]

son Stanley, who within months was appointed managing director, a post he was to hold for forty four years. Henry White Smith and Sydney Smith, his sister's sons also subscribed, becoming respectively secretary and manager of the Works. White's enthusiasm for the project is admirably encapsulated in a story told in *The People's Carriage*, published in 1974: "his instructions to Foreman Challenger. . . as to the removal of the buses from the Filton Sheds were so firmly emphasized by his tapping his umbrella on the ground that it snapped in two; he hurled the remnants across the yard adding, "we are going to build aeroplanes!" On the advice of Émile Stern, an agreement was signed with the Société Zodiac of Paris to manufacture their aeroplanes under licence. This was an attractive proposition, as the Voisin design came complete with a guarantee to fly.[114] It is noteworthy perhaps that the only two registered British aeroplane companies which could claim to predate that at Filton were Short Brothers and Handley Page. They had capital of £600 and £500 respectively.[115] Bristol had £25,000. Eleven months later, White increased the capital to £50,000 and by the close of 1911 increased it again to £100,000. "The B. and C.A.C. works proper would make most of our constructors green with envy," enthused *The Aero* correspondent after a visit in February 1911, "so beautifully are they planned and built, being, with I think only one exception, the only shops actually designed for aircraft work. They have fine roof lights, dead level concrete floors, and all those conditions which go to turn out the best quality work. . . During the last few years it has been my fate to see a good many aeroplanes in the making, some good, some mere death traps, but I have certainly never seen more beautifully selected material put into any machine, nor have I seen material more carefully and accurately worked. . . A sight one could probably not see anywhere else in England at present was to be seen in a special room, kept warm and dry and dust-free for the purpose, namely seven brand new Gnome engines in a row, all assembled and ready for use as soon as fixed in the machines. That alone represents something like £3,000 of capital. . ." Edward Everard's publicity brochure of the same date simply claimed the factory the largest in the world.

White was of a different generation and a different type to the other pioneers. He had no intention of devoting his every waking hour, as others did, to constructing one-off machines in which he could fly himself. Instead, after the failure of the Zodiac (which despite its high quality was too heavy to fly), he at once ordered the adaptation of a Farman design which would work. He brought the finest pilots from France, including Edmond, Tétard, Tabuteau and the great Henri Jullerot. He assembled a team of the the best designers he could find:

Grandseigne, Verespuy, Challenger, Prier and England. A little later in 1912, he took on perhaps the most colourful of all his early staff, Henri Coanda.

Coanda was the son of the Romanian Commander-in-Chief and was born in Bucharest in 1887. He was an accomplished violinist and one time pupil of the sculptor Rodin, whose powerful influence is clearly seen in a surviving example of his work, a bronze cast in Berlin. His interest in flight had led him first to construct a mock-up of a rocket-propelled aircraft in 1905 and later to study aeronautics in Paris. By October 1910, when still aged only 24, he had designed and built a revolutionary plywood-skinned aircraft, powered by the world's first ducted-fan engine. While running up the engine for ground trials, Coanda found the heat of his "turbo-propulseur" greater than he had expected. "I was worried in case the heat of the jet blast coming back set the aircraft on fire. For this reason I concentrated on adjusting the jet and did not realise that the aircraft was rapidly gaining speed. Then I looked up and saw the walls of Paris approaching rapidly. There was no time to stop or turn round and I decided to try and fly instead. Unfortunately I had no experience of flying. . .The plane seemed to make a sudden steep climb and then landed with a bump. First the left wing hit the ground and then the aircraft crumpled up. I was not strapped in and was fortunately thrown clear of the burning machine."[116] His lateral thinking and considerable ability were put to immediate good use at Filton, even though his large bow-ties, long hair and artistic temperament were regarded with some misgivings by his less flamboyant colleagues.[117]

White consolidated his position by obtaining the exclusive selling rights for Great Britain and the Colonies of arguably the best aero engine available at the time, the French Gnome. Between 1910 and 1912 he set up production lines of extraordinary complexity, manufacturing at least ten different types of aircraft.

As George Francis Train would have done, White brought his business to the notice of the public, with a spectacular flying display on the Bristol Downs. It ran for several days in November 1910 and despite awful weather was attended by thousands. *The Bristol Times and Mirror* reported every move. Writing on Friday 11th, its correspondent noted that Boxkite No. 14 had been completed only on the Wednesday evening before and had been brought to Bristol by road. Once the plane was rigged and despite heavy rain, the 20 year old Bristol-born pilot Leslie McDonald "made three very successful straight flights", with Jullerot as passenger on the third. Jullerot then took over and "rose with the grace of a bird" to 150 feet. "M. Jullerot expressed himself highly delighted with the Bristol Biplane," the correspondent

Filton, Bristol: "the only shops actually designed for aircraft work." The first large scale factory for aeroplane production in England, which by 1911 (the date of this photograph) was claimed to be the biggest in the world. The buildings still stand.

"Here at Filton four or five aeroplanes in various stages. . . meet the eye," said the Company's advertising brochure of 1911. The roughed-out pieces were brought from the Bristol Tramway saw-mills at Brislington, where "stacked from the ground to the roof, is material for. . . three to four hundred aeroplanes".

55

White, with his new pilots Maurice Tétard and Henri Jullerot on the Bristol Downs, in November 1910. In 1940, Jullerot sent his 1911 aerial log-book to White's grandson. He wrote "it will give you another proof of the sharp foresight your grandfather and your father had in making such a thorough job of what their and my contemporaries thought sheer madness."

Jullerot and White's son Stanley "preparing for flight" over the Clifton Suspension Bridge on Boxkite No. 14: 8.30 a.m, November 13th 1910. Stanley served as managing director of the aircraft works from 1911 until 1958, by which time the mach 2 stainless-steel "Bristol 188" was under construction. He died in 1963.

noted, "adding that though this was its maiden flight, nothing more could be done to improve it. Indeed he was so satisfied that he would trust himself in it anywhere." By the following Wednesday, such was the confidence in the machine, that White allowed his two nieces go aloft as passengers. Drama ensued as Hilda Smith's hat was torn from her head by the rush of wind and was cut to pieces by the propellor. "We have been on the roof today watching the flying," wrote one of the housemaids at Cotham House to her family in the Forest of Dean. "Sir G's two nieces went up one day. They have been flying over Clifton. . . are you coming to treat me in the Biplane? Only £5!"[118]

By Thursday 17th, the *Times and Mirror's* description of a flight over the Avon Gorge with Tétard at the controls was lyrical. White's aeronautical message had found its target. "On he sped, over rugged rocks and cliffs which spelt doom should his delicate craft fail him, to the Suspension Bridge. Here a picture was presented which will live long in the memory of those that saw it – the wonderful bridge and the aeroplane as gems of modern science in a natural setting of unrivalled beauty. . . one began to realise that flying for humans was no chimera of the imagination, but an accomplished fact."

Having demonstrated his product in Bristol, White turned to the world at large. He sent Farnall Thurstan (his nephew by marriage), to India in December 1910, with Jullerot as pilot. There spectacular flights were made, including one before the Viceroy. Most were made in the company of Sefton Branker, a young officer stationed in the sub-continent, who in later years as Sir Sefton Branker was to become Director of British Civil Aviation.[119]

He sent his nephew Sydney Smith with a delegation to Australia, to demonstrate the Boxkite to the military and to the Government. His chief pilot was a New Zealander, Joseph Hammond (whose former occupations had included gold-digging at Klondike, fur trapping in Alaska, and performing as a cowboy in Buffalo Bill's circus). Hammond broke both height and distance records and caused a sensation amongst the thousands who turned out to watch, wherever his flights were advertised. The effect of his arrival at the military camp at Liverpool on May 4th 1911, where he was met by Lord Dudley and General Gordon, was typical. "General Gordon afterwards issued a memo, in which he expressed his appreciation of the flight. 'I very much doubt,' he wrote, 'whether the science of flying has ever been demonstrated in a more telling and at the same time delightfully thrilling manner. As an object-lesson from a military point of view, too much cannot be said, and one and all in camp are now more than fully convinced of the part that aviation must necessarily play in the near future as a factor in war.' The opinion was freely expressed in camp that the result of the flight must be the formation of a Commonwealth aerial corps to work with the forces during their training."[120] Amongst the spectators at Melbourne, enthused by the demonstration, was an Australian motor mechanic, destined to make his own name famous in aviation: Harry Hawker. He had been noticed by Sydney Smith, who was concerned that he and his friends were "suspicious characters" hanging around the flying ground. With Hawker was Harry Busteed, who soon after joined the British and Colonial as a pilot.[121]

The celebrated aviator, Joseph Christiaens was so impressed by what he saw of Bristol products that he purchased two aircraft and set off with three other pilots to tour Singapore, Java, South Africa, the Argentine and Peru. He applied for and was granted the sole agency for the company in all the countries he visited.[122]

Meanwhile White made sales to the Spanish, the Italians, the Romanians and even, through Émile Stern and his nephew Henry White-Smith, to the Czar. He set up flying schools at Brooklands in Surrey, where A.V. Roe had made the first observed powered flight and at Larkhill on Salisbury Plain, where he rented a site and flying rights over 2,284 acres from the War Office. The acreage included Stonehenge itself and there, above and beside the monument, the new science of aviation was taught and developed. "Away it goes," wrote Charles Harper, moved to poetic heights by one of White's aircraft, "above the solitary places of the Plain, astonishing the coveys of partridges that fly low over the brooding landscape, and scaring the hare in her form with mortal dread of some new hawklike enemy. And as the sunlight strikes aslant upon its planes, it touches them at this angle to a whiteness that is more than white, and at that to a gleam that is transcendent gold. It becomes a thing of fairy beauty, contrasting strangely with the grey monoliths of Stonehenge, that mysterious survival from dim aeons of an unrecorded past."[123]

He established schools in Europe as well, in Halberstadt and Madrid. A new school on Bristol lines was opened at Mirafiore, and Bristol planes were used at Malpensa.[124] His aircraft entered competitions at home and abroad, including the celebrated Circuit of Europe race in 1911, which covered 1,025 miles and involved two crossings of the channel. "Sir George must have spent over half a million pounds on aviation before he got any return," wrote Sefton Branker in later years.[125]

White's old friend Sir James Clifton Robinson died suddenly, though appropriately perhaps, in the seat of a tramcar in America in November 1910. In the previous September, however, he had been offered the chairmanship of a projected company named AIR Stations

The past and the future converge. Jullerot sets out over the Clifton Gorge, with Brunel's Suspension Bridge in the distance and horse-drawn carriages beneath. Asked by a *Times and Mirror* correspondent if he had any fear, Jullerot shrugged his shoulders and replied "I am insured".

"A sight which rivalled in interest the recent eclipse of the sun." The first ever flight over Sydney, Australia in May 1911. Joseph Hammond pilots Bristol Boxkite No. 10 around the dome of the Queen Victoria Markets. No. 10 was so reliable that after 765 miles flight, it needed no repairs. The reserve machine White sent out was never unpacked from its box.

Ltd. "A.I.R.", the name of the parent company, was an acronym for "Aviation Investment and Research". AIR Stations was to invite on to its board Sir Charles Campbell (chairman of A.I.R.), Mr. Roger Wallace, the chairman of the Aerial League, and Lord Northcliffe. Its stated purpose was to open "in the principal towns of Great Britain, stations for the arrival and departure of Aeroplanes, so that aviators can fly from town to town, confident of finding accommodation for their aeroplanes." The stations would provide day and night-time landing facilities, sheds, repair shops, fuel, oil, road transport and accommodation.[126] Robinson and White had almost certainly discussed the merits of this scheme, not least because the memoranda of association which White had drawn up for the British and Colonial and the Bristol Aeroplane Companies in February had already allowed for the revolutionary concept of the carriage of "passengers and goods . . . in the air." There is no indication in Robinson's papers that he ever accepted the chairmanship of AIR Stations or that the scheme ever progressed beyond the theoretical stage. In any event, by February 1911 White had beaten them to it. "Filton is the present terminal of the chain of aeroplane stations established by the British and Colonial Aeroplane Company" reported Charles C. Turner in an article for *The Field*.[127] "The next station east is Amesbury, in the centre of the great military area, where the firm have a number of machines, and where daily instruction is given to officers of the British Army. . . Farther to the east is the school at Brooklands, and on the east coast is the station at Shellbeach. This chain of stations is the first of its kind established in this country, and it will this year become a regular flying course, over which 'Bristol' flyers will demonstrate the advantages of air travel." Britain's first airports had been established. If war had not been looming, mass passenger transport would surely have been White's next goal.

Instead, having attracted numerous individual army officers to the flying school and air station which he had so carefully sited beside the Larkhill army camp, White fought to have flying adopted by a very reluctant military establishment. For as the Special Correspondent of the *Army and Navy Gazette* warned, "the authorities in Berlin are rapidly adding to the strength in aeroplanes of the German Army, and appear resolved to lose no time in getting on level terms with their neighbours in the West."[128] The secret "X" Department, set up at Filton in 1911 to develop the military application of aircraft "those marvellous instruments of war" as M. Clementel had described them in the French War Minister's Budget of the same year,[129] worked on the inventions of Lieut Dennison Burney, including aerial torpedoes fired from guns, aircraft with inflatable wings and sea planes with hydrofoils.[130]

"Ancien et moderne. Monoplan 'Bristol' virage au-dessus de Stonehenge." A postcard for the French market illustrates the extraordinary technological advances which White orchestrated above and around the monument. Stonehenge stood on part of the 2,284 acres he rented at Larkhill, as a flying ground or "Air Station".

The sheds built by White at Larkhill, Wiltshire, in June 1910. Charles Harper, the journalist, advised readers to call them hangars, "a term that will doubtless become in a few years as well known as the once strange word 'garage' is now." The "hangars" became a centre for military flying and played a leading rôle in the 1911 Army manoeuvres. They still stand.

62

At a dinner in 1912, White set out his views in a prophetic speech. "The airplane is now acknowledged to be a necessary arm of war, and it behoves our government to bestir themselves if we are not to be left behind in the great race. For, believe me, during the next five years the Powers will call for thousands, if not tens of thousands, of airplanes, and the developments in their use for both military and naval purposes will be startling. . . In my opinion the possession of a strong fleet of airplanes by any country will be a dominating influence for peace."[131]

Perhaps White's greatest initial contribution to the war, when it came, was that 308 out of the 664 available pilots had been trained at Bristol Schools.[132] Then came more than 600 B.E.2 aircraft made in his factories to government order and some 376 Bristol Scouts which served in most theatres. The most famous of these was that flown by Capt. Lanoe G. Hawker of No. 6 Squadron, who succeeded in forcing down three two-seater enemy aircraft armed with machine guns, his own machine having only a single-shot Martini carbine, strapped obliquely to the starboard side. For this, Hawker was awarded the Victoria Cross. Three Scouts were flown from the deck of H.M.S. Vindex in anti-Zeppelin patrols, one was even launched from the upper wing of a Porte flying boat, in an attempt to counter the Zeppelin's ability to escape through rapid ascent.[133]

Some 130 Bristol M1 monoplanes followed the Scout, and went into military service throughout the war zone, from the Central Flying School to Basra. Six found their way to Chile. In 1918, one of these became the first aircraft to cross the Andes, climbing to over 13,000 ft.[134] Most celebrated of all, however, was White's Bristol Fighter, ultimately one of the most successful two-seater fighters in the First World War, whose first flight − on September 9th 1916[135] − was the last he was to attend at Filton.

By then, and despite a valiant fight, his failing health was beginning to overwhelm him. He was 62 years old and a widower. His beloved wife, Caroline Rose, had died painfully in November 1915, only months after they had moved to their final and most splendid house. This was the 17th century Old Sneed Park, whose land, now covered with houses, stretched out on both sides of the lower reaches of the River Avon. He was spending increasing lengths of time at Hollywood Tower, Cribbs Causeway, an elegant early 19th century house he had bought, extensively remodelled and furnished, as a wedding present for his son, Stanley in 1908.

At Hollywood, much of the planning for the aircraft works had taken place, for it was only a mile or so due west of Filton and an

The prototype Bristol Scout, February 1914. Harry Busteed the pilot, is deep in conversation with Kate, White's daughter-in-law. Nearly 400 Scouts were built and served in all theatres of war. This one sank in the Channel during the 1914 race from London to Paris and back, because the French ground crew had failed to refuel its reserve tank.

The most successful British two-seater fighter of the First War, the Bristol F2B. George V (on the step) visited the production line in November 1917, exactly a year after White's premature death. White's son, by now Sir Stanley, stands beside the King. Samuel, White's brother and successor as company chairman, looks on.

inevitable participant in the dramatic scenes with which aviation had come to be associated. "The large number of Bristolians who visited Filton on the evening of the 30th ult. in the hope of seeing some more flying had their journey rewarded by witnessing one of the finest flights M. Maurice Tétard has ever made in the vicinity. Rising a few minutes after 7 o'clock in the new Bristol racing biplane, a very swift looking machine, M. Tétard, after a few graceful circles over the Filton Works, swept away in the direction of Westbury. Passing close to Hollywood Tower, the residence of Mr. Stanley White, he continued on his course. . ."[136]

It was here, in the privacy of 'Webbs Brake' (the woodland water garden) and in the adjoining deeply-dug sheep dip, that hydrofoil models from the 'X' Department had been tested. It was here that Henri Jullerot circled in a Boxkite above the pram which contained George's newborn grandson, with a view (he later explained) to instilling in him a lifelong love of aircraft.[137] Stanley White's green and gilt morocco visitors' book survives and records not only the visits of Henri Jullerot ("leaving for India, 2/XII/1910"), but Émile Stern, Bertram Dickson, Gordon England, Graham Gilmour, Herbert Thomas, C. Dennison Burney ("venerable Atlantic Fleet"), Capt. Gilbert de Winkels ("airman, Roma"), James Valentine, Louis Breguet and many other celebrated names from the aviation world. Surviving also from Hollywood is perhaps one of the first airmail letters ever delivered. Written on fine white cotton wing fabric in Stanley White's hand, it appears to have been weighted and dropped from a great height onto damp ground. It reads "We shall be home to Dinner 7.30. Gilmour not going. . . so we shall have to put up with him tonight."

Despite the comfort of his family around him, the strains on White in 1916 were immense, not least because Bristol City Council, who had retained the right to re-acquire the tramway system they had gratefully handed over in 1875, were pressing hard to take back his empire. The Government, too, were threatening to upset his last great project, the Paravane, which had been the outcome of a £10,000 research project he had financed to develop designs by Burney and Commander Usborne at the secret 'X' Department.[138]

The paravane (or 'otter' as it came to be called in the Merchant Navy) was effectively an underwater aircraft, which could be towed on a steel hawser from the bow of a ship. Its original purpose was the destruction of enemy submarines, but by 1915, Burney had realised that it could be used just as effectively against tethered mines.[139] White, with the Government's and Admiralty's full approval, was about to assemble sufficient private capital to finance its mass

Celebration of a happy marriage. George and Caroline White, photographed in 1905. Caroline's death in 1915, exactly a year before his own, affected White deeply.

George and Caroline White's final home. Old Sneed Park, Bristol: a fine 17th century house much enlarged in the 19th century. Later known as Nazareth House, it survived them by some fifty years, before being torn down for redevelopment. A few damaged 17th century trees, from the once great yew walk which dominated White's garden, still stand as a memorial.

Hollywood Tower, Cribbs Causeway, near Bristol, photographed in 1908. This elegant Georgian house was Stanley White's home from 1908–1963. Almost within sight of Filton aerodrome and linked for fifty years by a private telephone line, it will forever be associated with the pioneering age of British aviation. Many great 20th century engineers, aviators and politicians visited it, from Jullerot to Robert Menzies.

production. The viability of the entire life-saving invention depended on the certainty of orders placed by the French and Russian Governments. But now the Admiralty had changed its mind without consultation and declared its intention to give the design free to all friendly powers.[140] "One of the outstanding features which induced me to undertake the business was the specific right of sale to the Governments of Russia and France which would be vested in me," he told the Admiralty. "I foresaw that in connectio 1 with the equipment of the British Merchant Shipping, to say nothing of other countries, there would be large manufacturing operations which would involve those forming the syndicate in heavy monetary obligations and that from the nature of the case, as no public issue could be thought of, I should have to bring in private capitalists, who would be materially influenced by evidence that not only had the British Navy generally adopted the patent of one of its officers, but that other Governments had also paid to acquire similar rights."[141] The top secret project of which he was perhaps most proud was teetering on the brink.

The Paravane, White's last great project, from an official illustration in his confidential file. Burney and Usborne's invention, towed from ships, could sever tethered mines from their moorings. Paravanes have saved thousands of tons of shipping and many lives.

In public George White still looked boldly towards the future and to the introduction of an extraordinarily far-sighted new scheme of employment which he was planning and which he described in a speech in October 1916. "In my own concern," he said, "I am looking forward with much hope to see if I cannot bring some scheme by which I can get men interested. Think of the success of any great business which could secure the heart and soul of every man working in the shop, as well as the employer. Why I could sweep the World if I had a few thousand men who were imbued with feelings of that kind, who had the same interest as I had myself in that business with the same determination to overcome difficulty. . . why should not the working men of this country consititute themselves in such a way that they may exercise their labours to the full by taking risks, or by taking a share in the business that they are working in? Then the best man would come to the top."[142] He vigorously attacked those who accused him of being anti-trade union, insisting that "there has been a tendancy to put in force a system of Collectivism, and in that way the individual talent, brain and handicraft of the individual mind has been swamped. . . There is a sort of opinion that I have views hostile to trade unionism. That is nothing of the kind! The only objection that I have to Trade Unionism is their policy of restriction of individual capacity. . ."

In private, things were different. "My Dear Sam," he had written to his brother from Old Sneed two months earlier, "I am tired out! I have devoted my life to work which in a year or two at most would result so successfully that you and I could square up with the world and neither of us be worried − but I get *so tired* I sometimes fear I shall not have the strength to carry it through − if not, you must do it old man. . . No one will ever know the anxieties poor dear Rose and I have gone through but I want you to know that all is well between you and I and that I am still your loving brother, George."[143]

He spoke similarly to his friends. "Twelve months ago," recalled J.H. Howell, just after White's death, "he sustained a heavy blow by the death of Lady White, and from that he never recovered. Last year on Colston Day when walking with him in the Dolphin Procession from the Cathedral. . . after alluding to the serious illness of Sir Henry Miles and the recent passing away of Sir Herbert Ashman (he) said 'I am going to be the third Bristol baronet to go out'. At the time, he (the speaker) thought his friend was a little low spirited, but no doubt he had some premonition of what his end was to be."[144]

That end came suddenly at Old Sneed on the evening of November 22nd 1916. He had chaired two meetings that day, one of the Main Colliery and, in the afternoon, of the Royal Infirmary. He had received a triumphant note from Burney about the Paravane, telling him ". . . that the treasury solicitors have reported that the Admiralty have no case and that you could legally claim pretty well what you liked. . . Unless we hear something very soon I think you might consider the advisability of placing an order for say 400 paravanes with some firm, as then that could be reported to the Admiralty & would help to commit them still further. . ." He had replied cautiously. "I suppose they will in due course send me some formal intimation of their proposals when you & I must meet to send reply – but I think it would be unwise to commit ourselves to an order . . . until we have a clear definition of the exclusive licence." He had then returned home and was working at his desk between nine and ten in the evening, when in an instant he fell forward and was gone. "Your telegram has indeed taken all the spirit out of me," wrote the matron of his hospital at Nice, to Stanley White. "To be removed like this seems unbelievable – what shall we do now?"[145]

St. Mary's Church, Stoke Bishop, Bristol, November 1916. White had wanted a simple funeral, but even so a sizeable crowd gathered. Here his coffin is carried towards the vault he had built for his wife's remains, twelve months earlier. Under the banner headline "Bristol's tribute to Sir George White", this photograph filled the front page of the London *Daily Sketch*.

70

In due course the Paravane was produced by Vickers, and saved countless thousands of lives.[146] "Here it falls to observe that the late Sir George White was a true patriot," wrote L. Cope Cornford in *The Paravane Adventure* (1919), "he was a pioneer in scientific aviation, and spent money and time in research and experiment, without thought of gain."[147] The Otter is still in use.

The hospitals to which he gave so much also continue their lifesaving work. His nationwide transport systems are still a way of life for many thousands of commuters and city dwellers. Numerous attempts have been made by the city of Bristol to reintroduce his tramways, which they had eventually acquired and abandoned. His stockbroking business, now merged with others, still flourishes. Many buildings he built or influenced still stand in Bristol, London and other cities. Amongst the finest Bristol examples are perhaps his Stock Exchange in St. Nicholas Street, the Edward VII Wing of the Bristol Royal Infirmary, the Tramway Depot at Brislington and the Counterslip power station by the Docks.

Countless thousands have enjoyed employment through his concerns, and still do. His aircraft works, now divided between British Aerospace and Rolls-Royce, is still the largest aeronautical site in Europe and has held a noble record in both war and peace. Concorde was primarily a Bristol design and first flew in England from his factory. Through Giotto, Hubble and other space projects, his tramlines now stretch to the stars.

"When the great aeronautical history of the world comes to be written," declared *The Aeroplane* on November 29th 1916, "his name will hold a foremost place among those who have made Britain's command of the air a possibility. As a pioneer of locomotion. . . his name will live for ever."

"He is succeeded in the baronetcy by his son George Stanley White," added the *Financial News*, "who has been largely instrumental in consolidating and enlarging the aeroplane enterprise, which is a monument to the foresight of a singularly able, amiable and modest man, whose greatest happiness was to be known as "of Bristol."[148]

Appendix I

SIR GEORGE WHITE 1ST BARONET
SIR GEORGE THE BRAVE.

His "Ever Watchful" Coat of Arms,
Proclaimed the man he proved to be.
Times of great stress and War's alarms,
Called forth his powers most strenuously.

He saw the coming of the Zep,
Our peaceful homes to violate.
Nor did he hesitate to step,
Into the breach to help the State.

With flying men and aeroplane,
Those "Bristol" planes with eagle eyes,
The outcome of his fertile brain,
His name and fame will immortalise.

He helped the poor to ride in state,
And build their homes on suburb soil,
They laugh and talk just tete-a-tete,
Nor fret nor fume about their toil.

In early days horses were yoked
To cars which ran upon the line,
Electric power he next evoked,
And power, light, speed did thus combine.

When he had knelt before our King,
To set the seal on work he'd done,
He set his heart on a gracious thing;
Yes, Charity he'd now enthrone.

72

Battles raged and men were maimed !

"Succour for the wounded" was the cry !
The Knight was there, Sir George the Brave,
The Red Cross Banners floated high,
The bandaged heroes' lives to save.

This well-meaning poem, though worthy of William McGonagall, is from *Historic Poems mostly relating to Bristol* by Charles Challenger: Bristol 1916. Challenger described himself as "Thirty seven years late traffic manager" of Bristol Tramways. He was father of George H. Challenger, the first engineer of the British and Colonial Aeroplane Company and designer of the Bristol Boxkite.

Appendix II

The Family of Sir George White Bt. (1854 – 1916)

Henry White of Honiton (b. 1787, d. 1862) = Elizabeth Tucker (b. 1811, d. 1863)

Henry White of Bristol (b. 1815 at Honiton, d. 1872 at Bristol) = Eliza Tippetts (b. 1818, d. 1906)

- Henry White (b. 1846) = Anne Susan Mants (emigrated to Sao Paulo, Brazil.)
- Elizabeth (b. 1848) = Edward Everard (and had issue)
- Georgina (b. 1851) = William George Smith (d. 1884)
- [Sir] George (b. 1854, d. 1916) = Caroline Rosina Thomas (b. 1854, d. 1915)
- Samuel (b. 1861) d. unm. 1928

From Georgina = William George Smith:
- [Sir] Henry White Smith (b. 1879) (had issue)
- [Col] Sydney Ernest Smith (b. 1881) (had issue)

From [Sir] George = Caroline Rosina Thomas:
- Daisy May White White (b. 1877)
- [Sir] (George) Stanley White Bt. (b. 1883, d. 1964) = Kate Muriel Baker

From [Sir] Henry White Smith:
- [Sir] William George Verdon Smith (b. 1876) = Diana Florence Anders
- [Sir] (William) Reginald Verdon Smith (b. 1912 d. 1993) = Jane Margaret Hobbs

From [Sir] (George) Stanley White:
- [Sir] George Stanley Midelton White Bt. (b. 1913 d. 1983) = Diane Eleanor Abdy Collins

From [Sir] (William) Reginald Verdon Smith:
- William George Verdon Smith. (has issue)
- *Elizabeth Jane Verdon Smith

From [Sir] George Stanley Midelton White:
- Daphne Eleanor White (has issue)
- [Sir] George Stanley James White Bt. (b. 1948) = *Elizabeth Jane Verdon Smith

From [Sir] George Stanley James White = *Elizabeth Jane Verdon Smith:
- George Philip James White b. 1987

74

Notes

1 *Bristol Guardian*, November 24th 1916.
2 *Bristol Guardian*, December 2nd 1916.
3 *Western Daily Press*, November 18th 1916.
4 *Bristol Times and Mirror*, November 27th 1916. The preacher was Canon Everingham, acting as Bishop's Messenger.
5 Undated cutting, Family Archive.
6 *Marriage and Baptism Records* of Cullompton and Honiton. Address given 1841 *Census Return* [PRO HO 107/200].
7 Martin Smith: *The Railways of Bristol & Somerset* [Ian Allan Ltd., Surrey 1992] p. 8.
8 Dates and facts from the *Marriage Record* of St. George's Brandon Hill, also the *Census Return*, Parish of St. Michael, Bristol, 1841 [PRO HO 107/1951].
9 *Baptism Records*, Parish of St. Michael, Bristol.
10 G.E. Cummings (attrib.): *Sir Clifton Robinson Deceased* [Manuscript biography c.1910] Chapter III (addition) p. 7. Family Archive.
11 Ibid p. 8.
12 Speech on War Bonus at Brislington Saturday October 14th 1916. Family Archive.
13 Cummings [op. cit.] p. 8.
14 Bristol Records Office: Acc. No. 35810 GW/C/8 Letter from Henry White March 6th 1889.
15 T.W.H. Gailey: Chapter I, *The People's Carriage* [Bristol Omnibus Company 1974] p. 4.
16 *Zig-Zag*, February 24th 1881.
17 Charles Harvey & Jon Press: *Sir George White of Bristol* [Bristol Branch of the Historical Association, Pamphlet No. 72 1989 p. 3].
18 College of Arms: *Pedigree of Sir George White*. Family Archive.
19 Edward Everard: *A Bristol Printing House* [Edward Everard, Bristol, undated, p. 51].
20 Everard [op. cit.] p. 9.
21 *Marriage Register*, Moray Church, Edinburgh.
22 College of Arms: *Pedigree of Sir George White*. Family Archive.
23 Bristol Records Office Acc. 35810 GW/A/4: payment for ground rent, Jan. 1st 1876, also 35810 GW/A/1 receipt for ground rent Jan 12th 1876.
24 B.R.O. MS 35810 GW/A/5b: Bank Book.
25 B.R.O. MS 35810 GW/A/1: letter 10th Jan 1876.
26 B.R.O. Acc. No. 35810 GW/A/1.
27 Cummings [op. cit.] Chapter 3 p. 9.
28 B.R.O. Acc No. 35810 West of England and South Wales District Bank Book Dec. 31st 1876–Dec. 7th 1878.
29 Cummings [op. cit.], Chapter II, p. 2.

30 B.R.O. Acc. No.35810/J.C.R./P/4 letter to Hon. G.F.Train dated Feby 3rd.
31 *The New York World*, Sunday October 12th 1902.
32 Cummings [op. cit.] pp. 16–17.
33 Cummings [op. cit.] Chap. 3 p. 6.
34 Cummings [op. cit.] Chap. 3, p. 15.
35 *Zig-Zag*, February 24th 1881.
36 *Yorkshire Observer*, November 24th 1916.
37 B.R.O. Acc. No. 35810 GW/T/21 p. 30.
38 *The Magpie*, March 8th 1890.
39 *Bristol & London and South West Junction Railway: Minutes of Evidence* 1883.
40 Harvey & Press [op. cit.] p. 10.
41 Stories of George White's business coups are frequently repeated in contemporary articles, especially obituaries, but are clearly and accurately reported with reference to primary records by Harvey and Press [op. cit.].
42 The author is grateful to the private collector from whose archive this information is taken.
43 *The Magpie*, March 8th 1890.
44 Harvey and Press [op. cit.] p. 12.
45 For example: *Bristol Times & Mirror*: Nov. 28th 1916 "Operations on a large scale naturally made him a power in the West of England, and his support was as much appreciated as his criticism was feared."
46 See *The Journal of the Corris Railway Society*, 1990, p. 19.
47 See Geoffrey Wilson: *London United Tramways* [London 1971].
48 Edited by Clifton Robinson, printed for L.U.T. during the year 1898. A sister newspaper bore the name *Ealing Election News*.
49 Preface to a bound volume of the *Ealing Election News* and *Chiswick Electric Tramways News*.
50 P. Smith & M.J. Powell: "Calico, Creosote and Colliers" *Bristol: The Growing City* [Redcliffe: Bristol 1986].
51 London United Tramways: *Souvenir of the Inauguration of the Company's Electric Tramways* London 1901.
52 London United Tramways: *Souvenir of the opening for Public Traffic etc.* London 1901 and L.U.T: *Souvenir of the Inauguration of the Company's Electric Tramways*, London 1901.
53 Citation survives. Family Archive.
54 Cummings [op. cit.]: Ch. 13: "A Deal and its Consequences." See also A.A. Jackson & D.F. Croome: *Rails through the Clay* [London 1962]. pp. 83–85.
55 Wilson [op. cit.] p. 84.
56 Wilson [op. cit.] pp. 85–86.
57 Jackson & Croome: [op. cit.] p. 84.
58 The other reason was his wife's delicate health. His brother Henry had written from Brazil (March 27th 1892) "I am awfully sorry that Rose has been so ill, we all had no idea of it. . . you don't say what is the

matter with her, but as you are going to the south of France I fear it is something to do with her lungs. . ." [B.R.O. 35810 GW/C/8].

59 J. Wright & Co., *Bristol Directory* 1880.
60 Birth certificate of George Stanley White (copy dated December 13th 1916).
61 *The Bristol Magpie*, March 8th 1890: "Last year Mr. White gave up his house at Stapleton where he is much missed by the villagers, and having purchased the Cotham House Estate (so long occupied by Mr. Samuel Budgett) has taken up residence at this charming and historical spot."
62 B.R.O. Acc. No. 35810 GW/C/9 Feb. 7th 1890.
63 B.R.O. Acc. No. 35810 GW/A/9, Jan. 2nd 1891.
64 B.R.O. Acc. No. 35810 GW/A/9 Bill from Charles Trapnell for "attending cow and medicine".
65 Loose inventory pages. Family Archive.
66 B.R.O. Acc. No. GW/C/1a: Letter to North British & Mercantile Assurance Co. Feb. 10th 1904.
67 R.P. Way *Antique Dealer* [Michael Joseph, 1956] p. 44.
68 Cutting from *The Gentlewoman*, "Lady White at Home", 1905. Family Archive.
69 Bill totalling 11,000 francs for this and other items. June 14th 1904. Family Archive.
70 "We are enabled to reproduce in the present number, through the courtesy of Sir George White, Bart., a most interesting portrait of *Napoleon in Egypt*, by Edouard Detaille, the noted military painter, which hangs at Cotham House, at Bristol. The plate is reproduced from blocks made by Mr. Edward Everard, of Bristol, who made them specially for Sir George White. . ." *The Conoisseur*, 1908.
71 A letter written by G.W. to his insurers (June 27th 1904) states that the third row of pearls alone cost £4,222.10.0 when bought from Messrs. Hunt & Roskell, London. [B.R.O. 35810 GW/C/1a]. See also *A casket of Important Jewels, the property of the late Sir George White Bart.* Christie, Manson & Woods, Wednesday January 31st 1917.
72 Cutting from a local newspaper. Source unknown. Family Archive.
73 Cutting from a local newspaper, probably the *Western Daily Press*. Family Archive.
74 Family Archive.
75 B.R.O. Acc No. 35810 GW/C/8/, March 6th 1889 and Feb. 7th 1890.
76 Family Archive. Letter dated January 7th 1902.
77 *Financial News*, Nov. 24th 1916.
78 Letter dated Aug. 2nd 1904. Family Archive.
79 John Mathieson "The Years of Expansion", *The People's Carriage* [Bristol 1974] p. 65.
80 *The Financial News*, Thursday July 30th 1903. Also *The Bristol Times and Mirror* of the same date.
81 *British and American Hospital 1906–1956*. Family Archive.
82 December 22nd 1906.

83 G. Munro Smith: *History of the Bristol Royal Infirmary* [Bristol 1917] p. 416.
84 *Western Daily Press*, December 22nd 1916.
85 B.R.O. Acc. No. GW/C/12, March 30th 1905.
86 Carnival Programme. Family Archive.
87 June 29th 1905.
88 B.R.O. Acc No. 35810 GW/C/12: March 19th 1905.
89 B.R.O. Acc. No. 35810 GW/C/12: March 28th 1905.
90 Munro Smith [op. cit.] p. 417.
91 Tom Twain: *The Bristol Magpie*, June 29th 1905.
92 Munro Smith [op. cit.] p. 418.
93 Andor Gomme, Michael Jenner and Bryan Little: *Bristol, an Architectural History* [Lund Humphries, London. 1979] p. 414.
94 Souvenir Programme. Family Archive.
95 *Western Daily Press*, June 29th 1912.
96 *Bristol Times and Mirror*, November 24th 1916.
97 C. Bruce Perry: *The Bristol Royal Infirmary* [Portishead Press, 1981] p. 30.
98 A ward in the old building named the White Ward may, perhaps relate to the family.
99 *Financial Times*, February 1910.
100 The Mercedes Records show that Samuel White's car was delivered in March 1903. It apparently had a rear-entrance tonneau body and was ordered through William S. Hogan of 31 Avenue Kleber, Paris. (The author is indebted to David Hales for this information.)
101 The Panhard was collected from Paris by Stanley White and driven back to Bristol. It had arrived by July 31st 1903.
102 For example B.R.O. Acc. No. 35810 GW/C/1c: October 31st 1905 and November 27th 1905. Also GW/C/1/i, February 15th 1908.
103 20 h.p. chassis bought August 1904 (B.R.O. Acc. No. GW/C/1/i). For the 75 h.p. chassis, see footnote 110.
104 P. Hulin: "Bristol's Buses", *The People's Carriage* [op. cit.] p. 31.
105 Hulin [op. cit.] p. 32.
106 Allen Janes & Phil Sposito: *Bristol Goods Vehicles* [Whitchurch c. 1989.]
107 Ibid. p. 32.
108 Ibid. p. 32.
109 Ibid. p. 33.
110 B.R.O. Acc. No. GW/C/1/i. Letter from G.W. to Messrs. Kellner & fils, 125 Avenue Malakoff, Paris: "with reference to the limousine body which you are fitting to the 75 h.p. Léon Bollée chassis, I understand from Mr. Stern that the work is now finished. . ."
111 John Pudney: *Bristol Fashion* [Putnam 1960] p. 22.
112 John Mathieson [op. cit.] p. 64.
113 C.H. Barnes: *Bristol Aircraft since 1910* [Putnam 1964] p. 13.
114 Barnes [op. cit.] p. 45.
115 Peter King: *Knights of the Air* [Constable 1989] pp. 64 & 67.

116 *The History of Aviation* ed. J.W.R. Taylor and K. Munson [London 1978] pp. J88D89.
117 Reported to the author by his grandmother, the Dowager Lady White.
118 Family Archive.
119 John Pudney: *Bristol Fashion* [Putnam 1960] pp. 59–61.
120 *The Australian Daily Telegraph*, May 4th 1911.
121 Pudney [op. cit] p. 62.
122 *Bristol Aeroplanes*. A publicity brochure of the Company [Edward Everard, 1911] p. 11.
123 Charles G. Harper: *The Outlook*, February 11th 1911.
124 Barnes [op. cit.] p. 21.
125 John Pudney [op. cit.] p. 54.
126 B.R.O. Acc. No. 35810 GW/T/34 a, b. September 3rd 1910.
127 *The Field* No. 3032, February 4th 1911. (The report was taken almost word for word from the B & C.A.C's own brochure.)
128 *The Army and Navy Gazette*, February 4th 1911. The cutting from which this quote is taken belonged to George White himself.
129 *The Field* No. 3032 [February 4th 1911].
130 Later Admiral Sir Dennison Burney and designer of the airship the R100.
131 *The Daily Express*, February 17th 1936.
132 Barnes [op. cit.] p. 24.
133 Barnes [op. cit.] p. 95.
134 Barnes [op. cit.] p. 122.
135 George White's office diary: 1916. Family Archive.
136 Newspaper cutting of unknown provenance, pasted in a scrapbook belonging to the (then) Mrs. Stanley White. The aeroplane described was probably a Boxkite variant (No. 44), first flown by Tétard on May 30th 1911 and flown subsequently by him in the Circuit de l'Europe air race.
137 George's grandson, George S. M. White (later the 3rd baronet) was told this story by Jullerot himself in 1940. As a reminder of these early events at Hollywood, a considerable collection of spars and skids, including a fragment of one of the "Zodiac" biplanes were discovered in the farm buildings during the 1960s.
138 Burney file. Family Archive.
139 L. Cope Cornford: *The Paravane Adventure* [London 1919] p. 87.
140 Burney file. [op. cit].
141 Burney file. [op. cit].
142 Speech on War Bonus, Brislington, Saturday 14th October 1916. "I believe in a system by which a man shall be paid for what he proves himself to be worth. That is the only cause for complaint or grumble I have with the Trade Union System of this Country. I do not like the idea of bringing every man down to a common level and that level a minimum level. Change it and set a high standard and make that the level, and let every man work up to it. . ."

143 July 15th 1916. Family Archive.
144 *Western Daily Press*, November 24th 1916.
145 Family Archive.
146 *Western Daily Press*, January 10th 1919: "From the day when the use of the Paravane became general only two cases of warships sunk by mines have been reported."
147 Cope Cornford [op. cit.] p. 16.
148 *Financial News*, Nov. 24th 1916.

Registered Charity No: 1010632

In June 1990, an initiative was launched in Bristol to commemorate the extraordinary achievements in aircraft production in the city from 1910 until the present day. Known as The Bristol Aero Collection, its intention is to set up the first museum of aircraft production in Great Britain, using the products of the Bristol Aeroplane Company, its predecessors and its successors, as its theme. The primary purpose is to provide an educational establishment to encourage enthusiasm for aviation and engineering in the young and to use the past for the benefit of the future.

The collection consists of a rapidly growing number of artefacts. These include a replica 1914 Bristol Scout, a replica 1919 Bristol Babe, a Bristol Britannia airliner, a Bristol Sycamore helicopter, a Bristol Bloodhound missile and a mock-up Giotto satellite kindly presented by British Aerospace, together with a wealth of smaller artefacts, an archive and a library. It is hoped that one day a permanent site will be found for them close to Filton aerodrome, where the industry started.